I0448327

Guitar Thesaurus
Vol.III Harmonization
by Stefanos Nikas

"You can't wait for inspiration, you have to go after it with a club."

*Many thanks to **Tasos Asonitis** for the help and support he provided me.*

Cover Photo by Haris Bampouras

First Edition

ISBN: 978-1-312-59206-3

All diagrams created using  **NECK DIAGRAMS**

Table Of Contents

Introduction

Suppose there is someone who wants to learn a very unique language. For a teacher, the proper instructional method would be to begin with the alphabet, then continue with vocabulary and grammar rules and finally show how to form full sentences in that language. "Guitar Thesaurus Vol.I & Vol.II" provides the practicing guitarist with all the vocabulary that he would ever come across while exploring the guitar universe. But as soon as someone learns the vocabulary, he has to be able to use it to speak in his own way.

"Guitar Thesaurus Vol.III: Harmonization" is about taking the scales examined in the previous volumes and creating chords that are built within these scales. It is also a handy guide for you to make your own songs, chord progressions and rhythm accompaniments.

Harmonizing a scale means taking every degree of it and using it as a tonic to build chords off the diatonic pattern of the particular scale tones. For example, the commonly used A Natural Minor scale creates (in consecutive order of 7ths) Am7, Bm7b5, Cmaj7, Dm7, Em7, Fmaj7 and G7. As always in the "Thesaurus Series" we do not confine ourselves by including only the widely known scales of the Major Family (Dorian, Phrygian, Lydian etc.). We take it a step further by providing the harmonization for every scale of the Harmonic Minor and Melodic Minor Family as well. That means that within your hands you are holding the chord patterns for more than 20 scales, including all those scales that are used in the more complex jazz tunes, like Lydian Dominant, Mixolydian b6, Dorian #4, Locrian #6, Phrygian Dominant, Ultralocrian and many more.

One more thing that makes Vol.III an addition to the previous series is the harmonization process which is applied in triadic, 7th, 9th, 11th and 13th chords providing you with all the possible colors and extensions that occur within every scale, always in the most efficient finger shapes. Once again, we stick with the movable grips to make the presented chords applicable to every key.

So, here pops the question. How should someone use "Guitar Thesaurus Vol.III"? As mentioned before, this guide is about taking the knowledge presented thoroughly in Vol.I & Vol.II and applying it to a practical context. Simply, choose the sound "texture" of your desire, find the scale that suits best, open the book on the corresponding pages and go creative with all the different options! Now you are able to compose anything, from rock songs to sophisticated jazz progressions without the need of a complex theoretical background.

Once again, we are happy to have included two bonus sections for all of you practice freaks out there. This time, the bonus segment includes 4-notes-per-string scales and 3-octave arpeggios.

There is no need for wasting any more time. Within the following pages lie the secrets of the most unique and beautiful language ever spoken by humans - Music. This guide along with your personal creativity are the only things you need in order to further develop your musical expression.

Stefanos Nikas
&
Tasos Asonitis

Reading Diagrams

High E String

A Major Scale

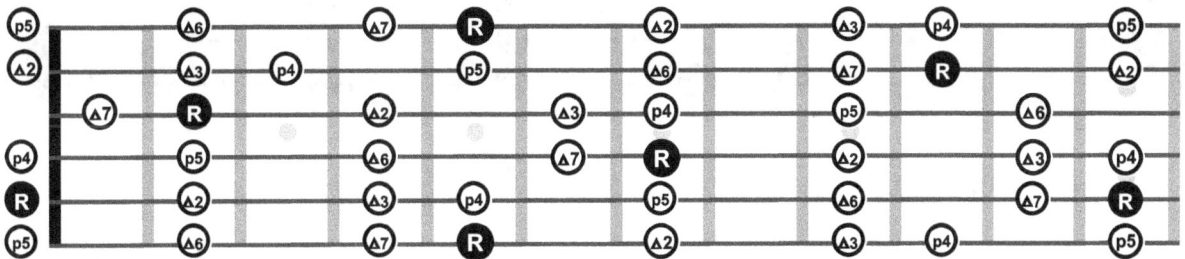

Nut

Root Note

Interval

Low E String

A

Root Note

Barre

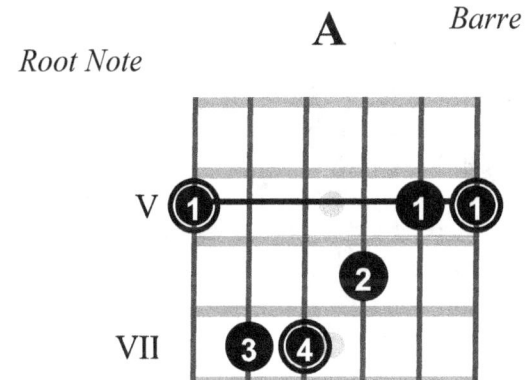

Finger Number

Muted String

Bm

Fret Number

Notes

R	=	Root
b2	=	Minor 2nd
Δ2	=	Major 2nd
b3	=	Minor 3rd
Δ3	=	Major 3rd
b4	=	Diminished 4th
p4	=	Perfect 4th
b5	=	Diminished 5th
p5	=	Perfect 5th
b6	=	Minor 6th
Δ6	=	Major 6th
bb7	=	Diminished 7th
b7	=	Minor 7th
Δ7	=	Major 7th

"All shapes are movable. They can be played anywhere on the fretboard depending on what key you are playing in."

A Major Scale

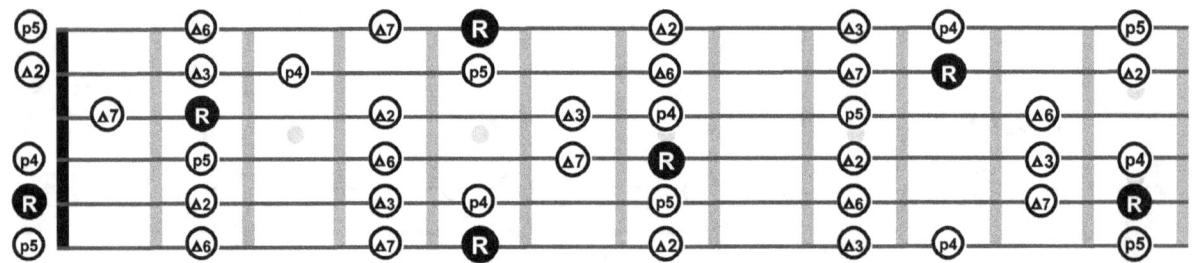

Triad Chords:

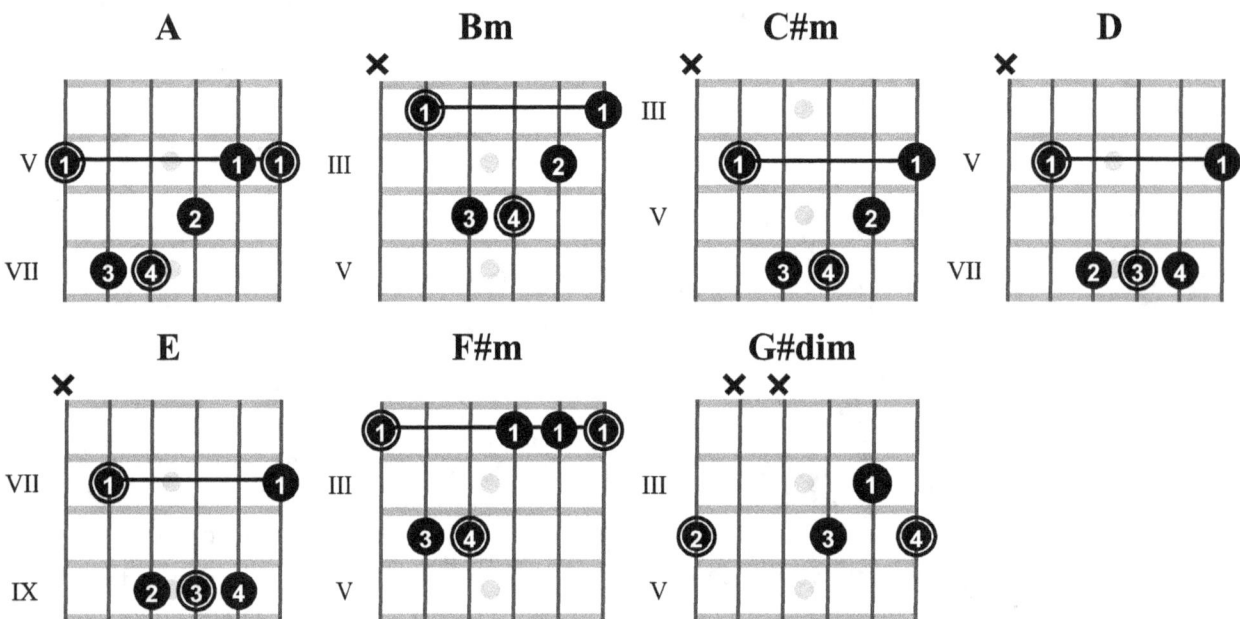

7th Chords:

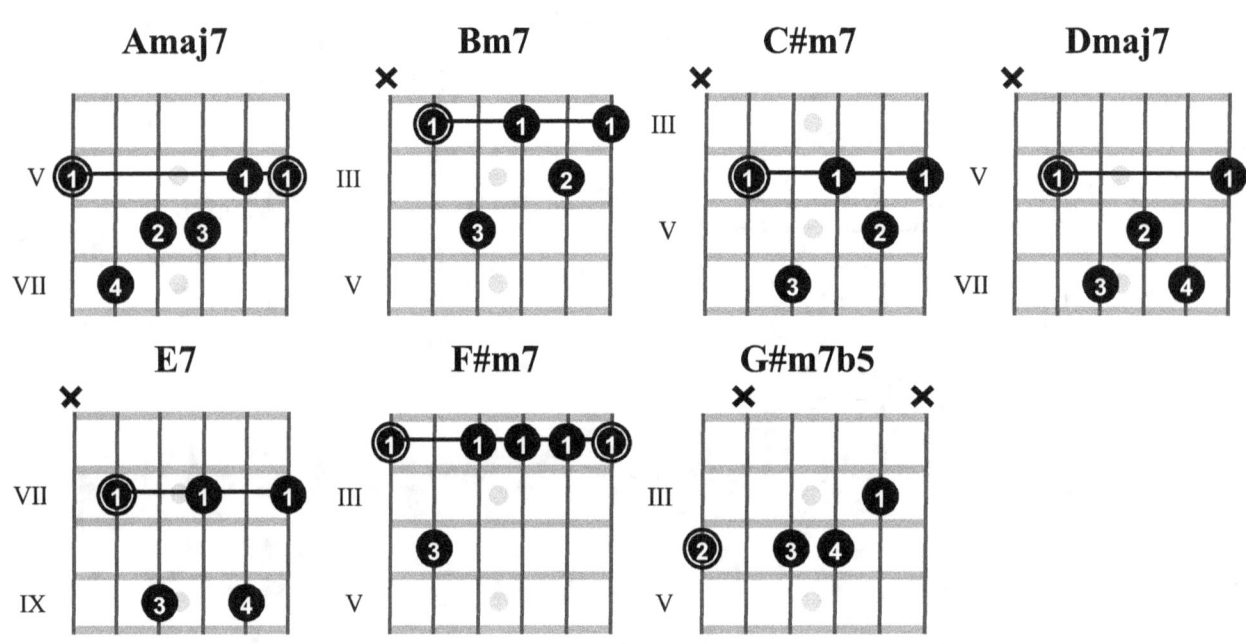

A Major Scale
continued

9th Chords:

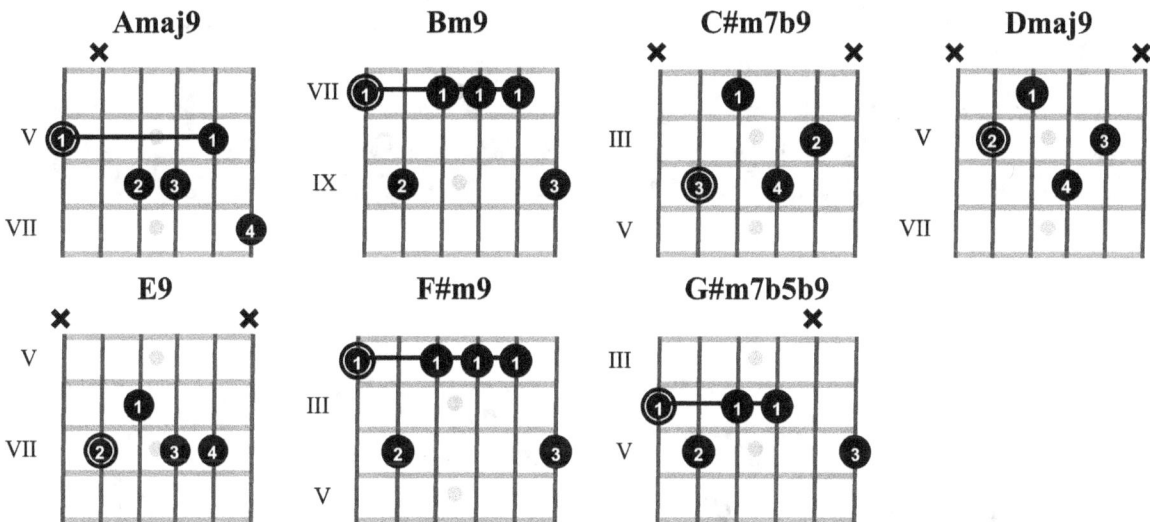

Amaj9   Bm9   C#m7b9   Dmaj9

E9   F#m9   G#m7b5b9

11th Chords:

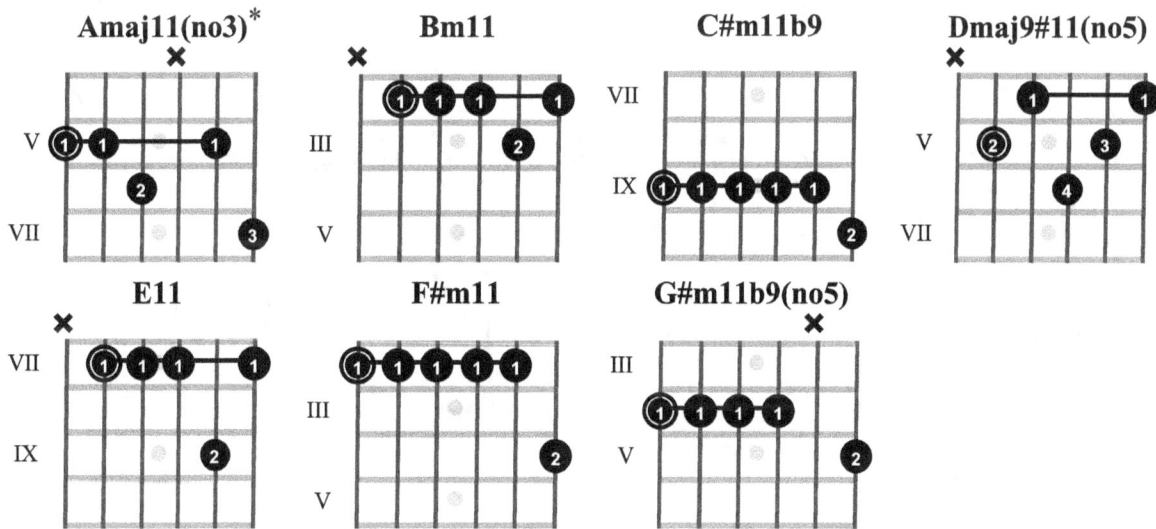

Amaj11(no3)*   Bm11   C#m11b9   Dmaj9#11(no5)

E11   F#m11   G#m11b9(no5)

13th Chords:

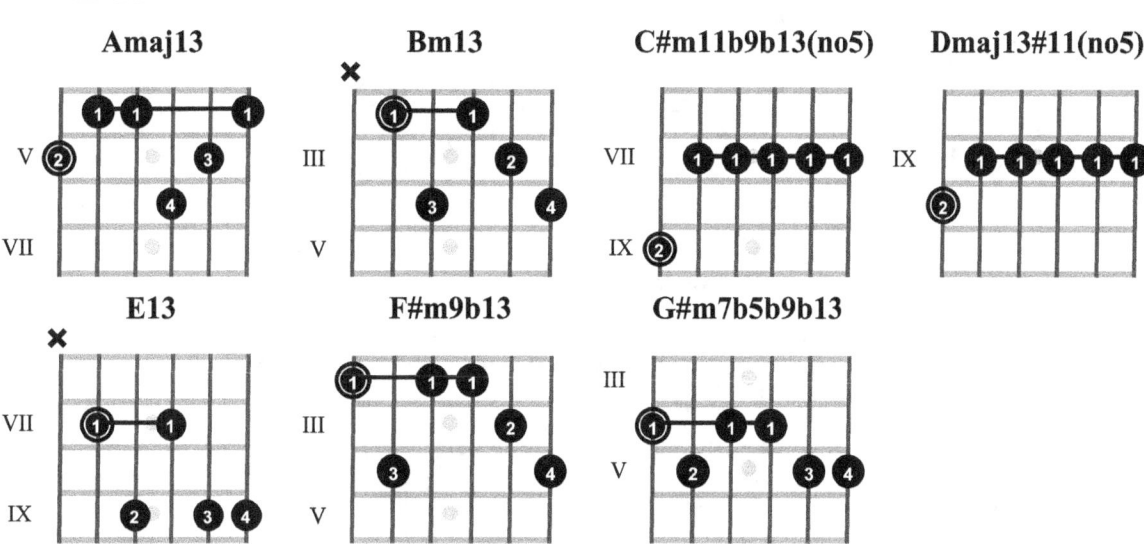

Amaj13   Bm13   C#m11b9b13(no5)   Dmaj13#11(no5)

E13   F#m9b13   G#m7b5b9b13

"The chord maj11 is almost never played with the major 3rd and the 11th (perfect 4th) sounding together. As you can see in this shape, the 3rd is excluded."

A Natural Minor Scale

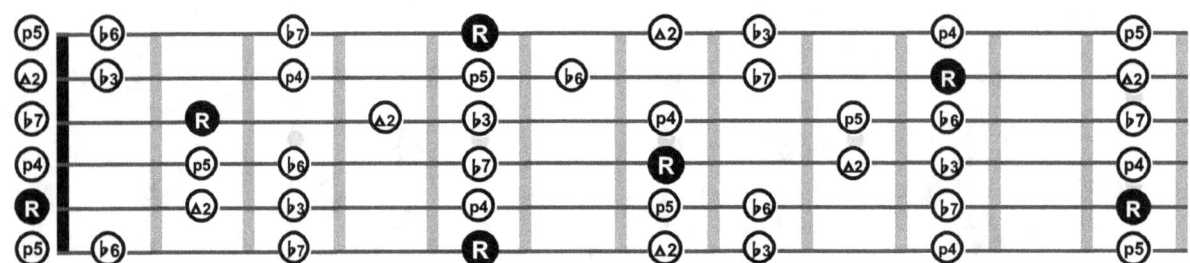

Triad Chords:

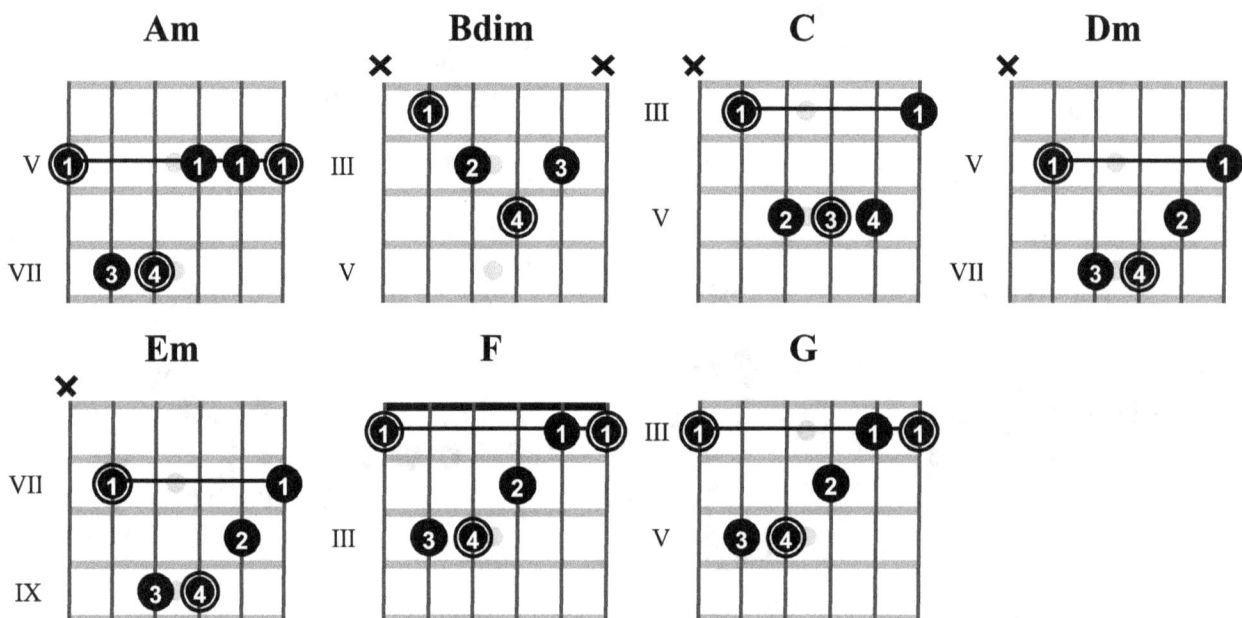

7th Chords:

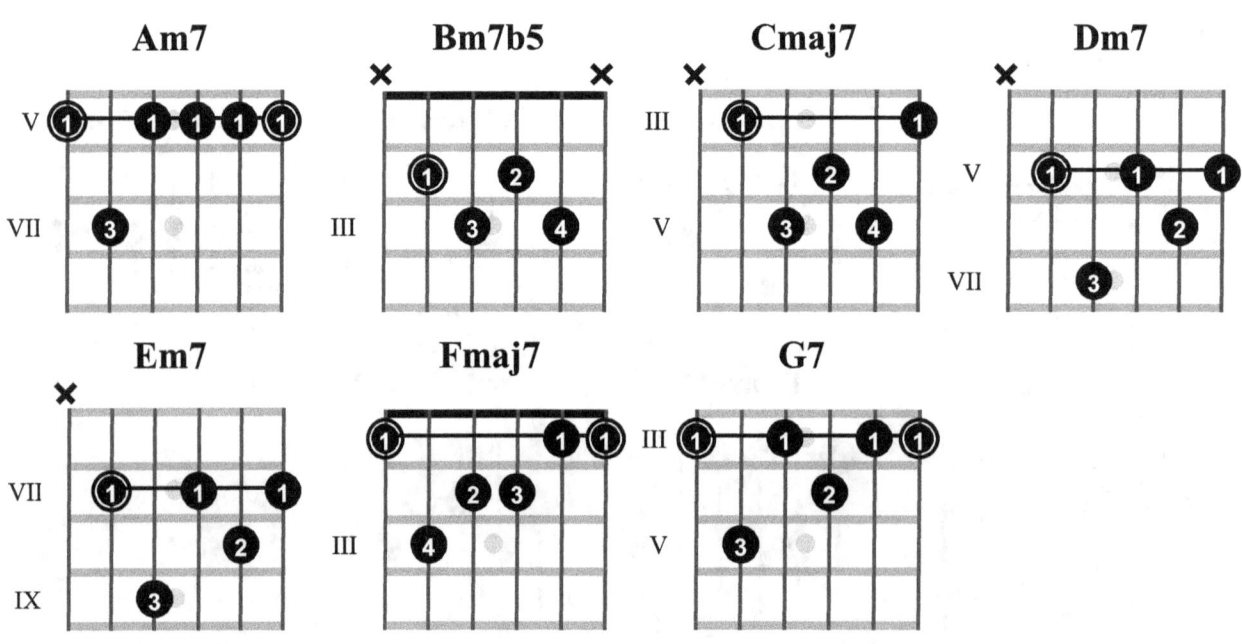

A Natural Minor Scale
continued

9th Chords:

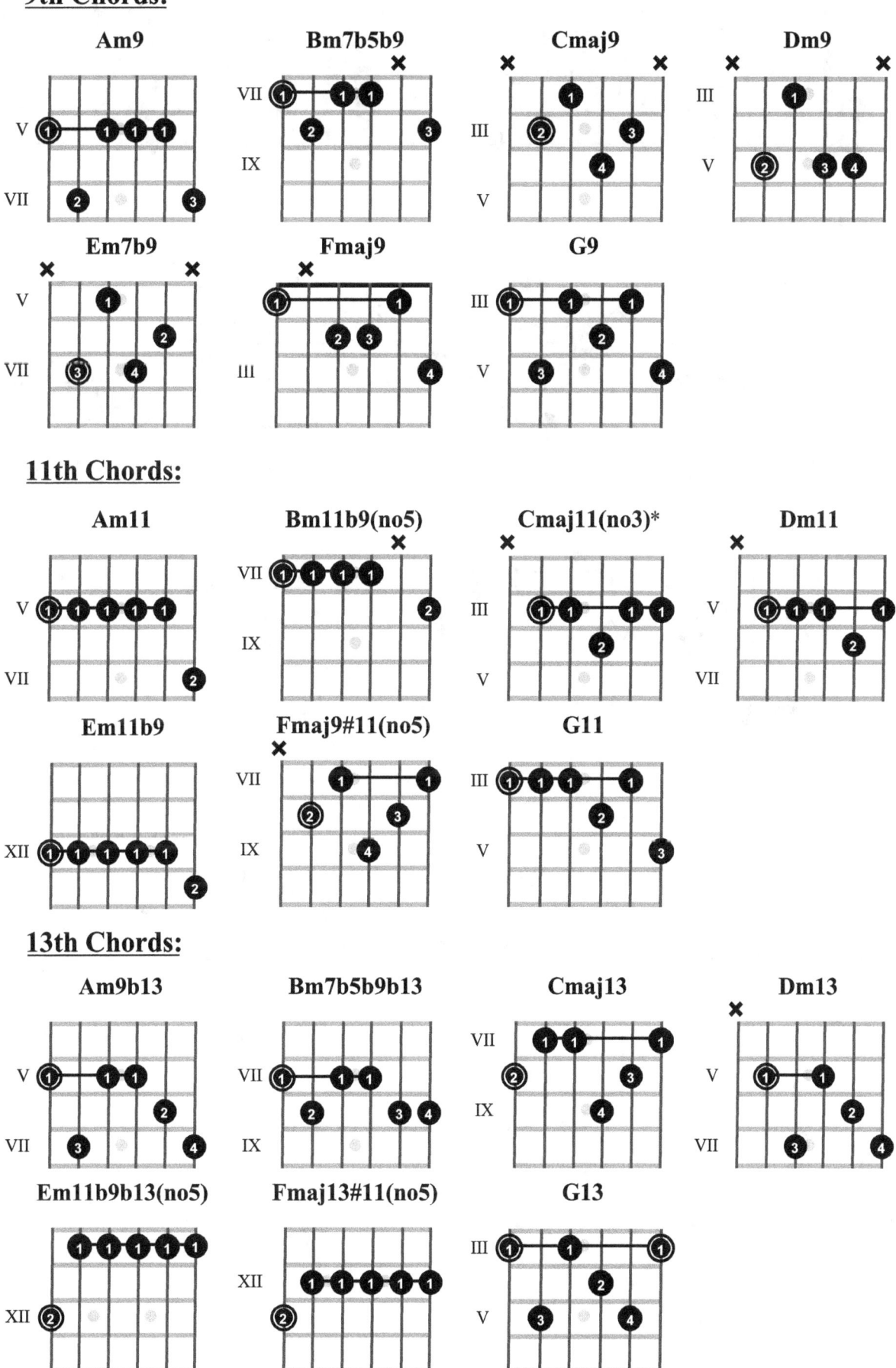

Am9   Bm7b5b9   Cmaj9   Dm9

Em7b9   Fmaj9   G9

11th Chords:

Am11   Bm11b9(no5)   Cmaj11(no3)*   Dm11

Em11b9   Fmaj9#11(no5)   G11

13th Chords:

Am9b13   Bm7b5b9b13   Cmaj13   Dm13

Em11b9b13(no5)   Fmaj13#11(no5)   G13

A Dorian Scale

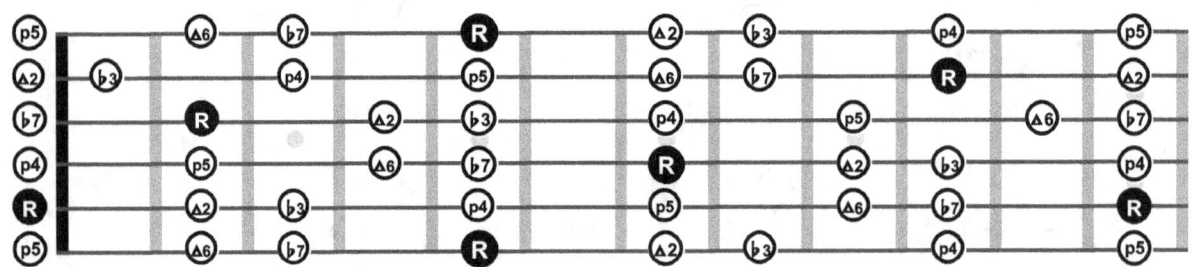

Triad Chords:

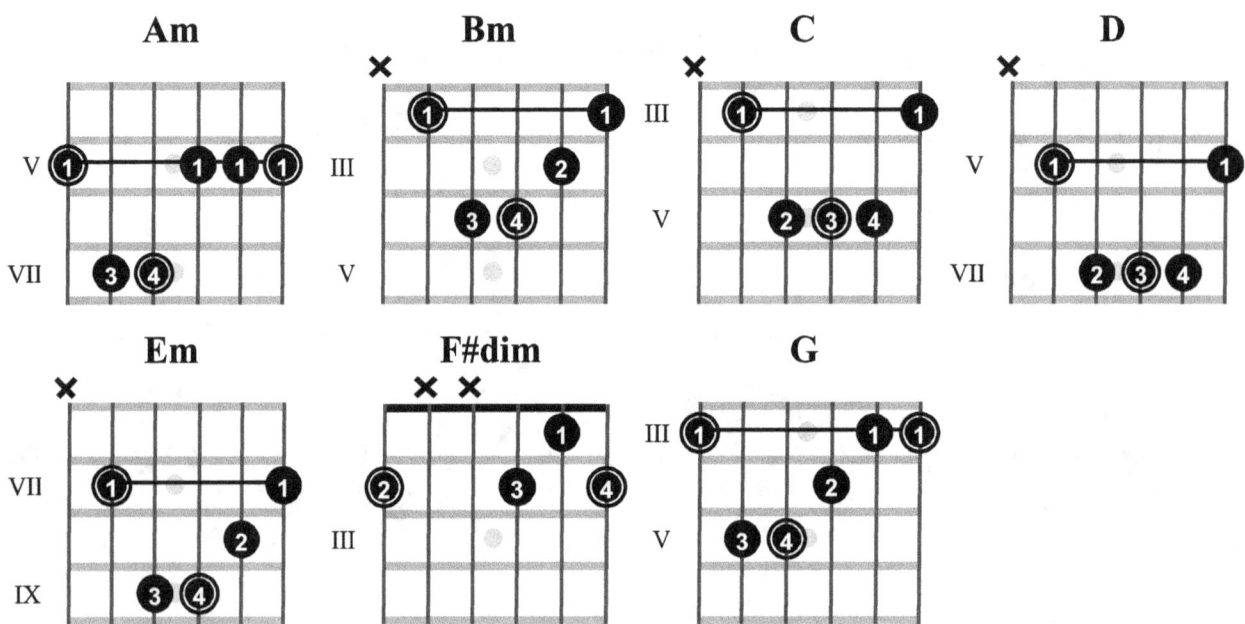

7th Chords:

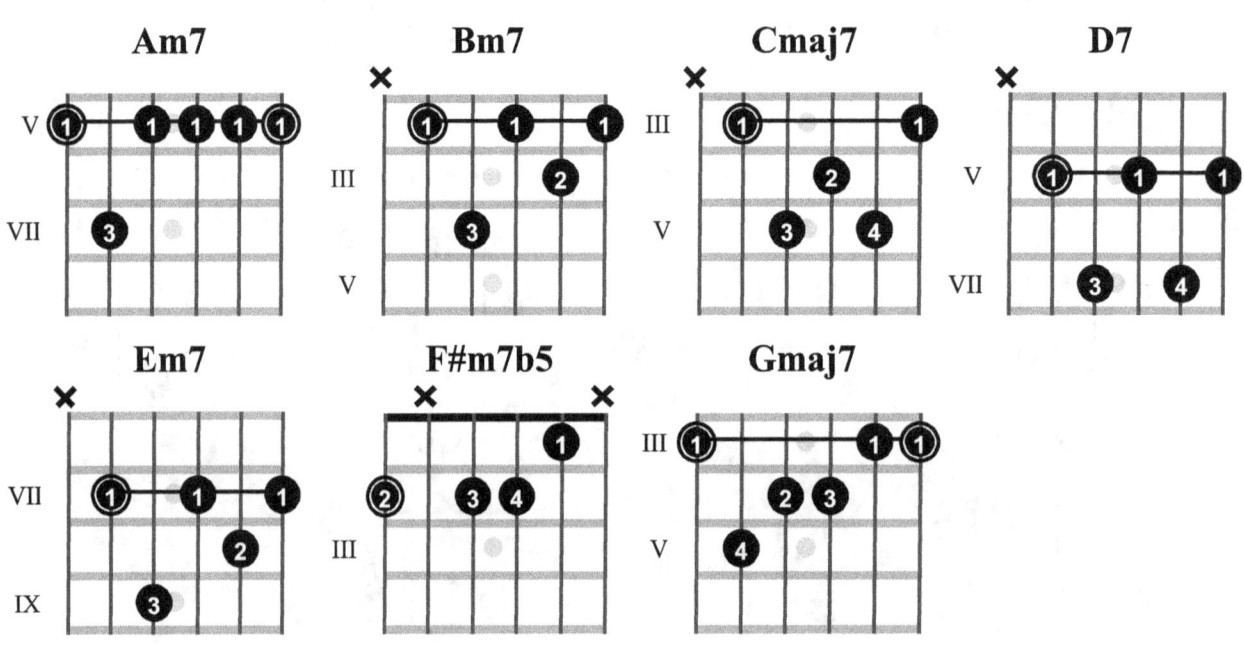

A Dorian Scale
continued

9th Chords:

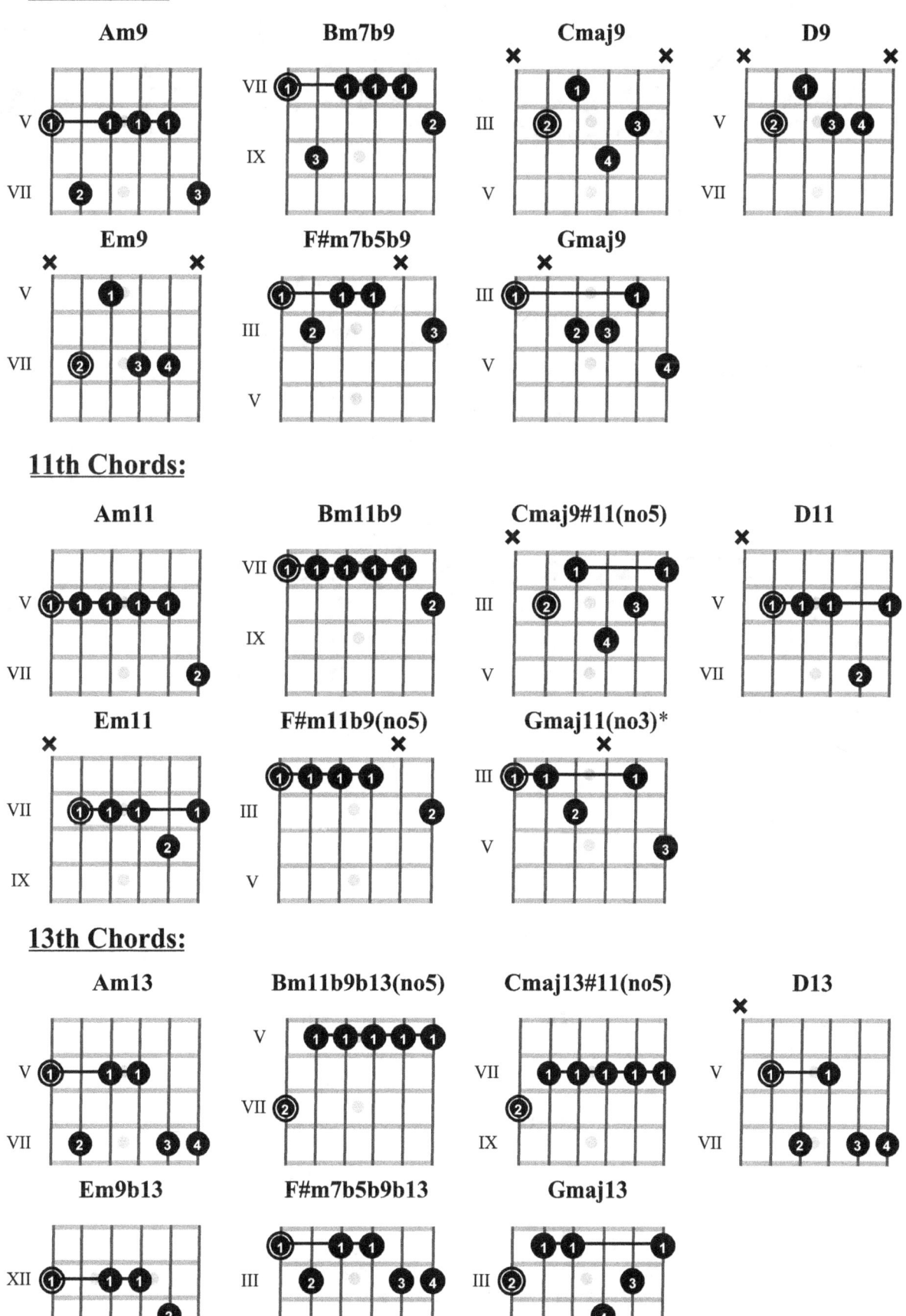

11th Chords:

13th Chords:

A Phrygian Scale

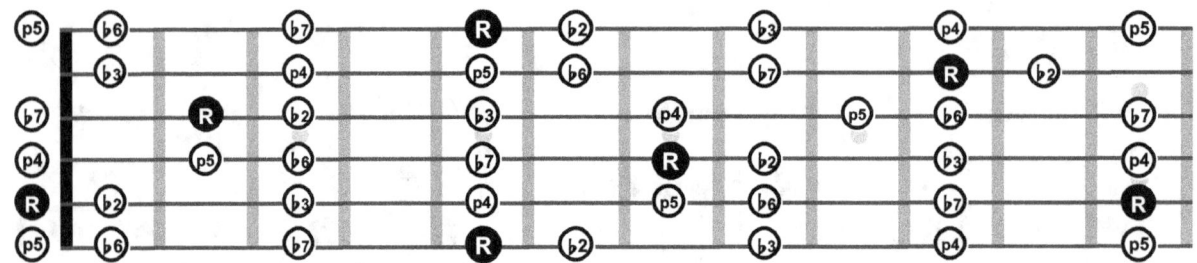

Triad Chords:

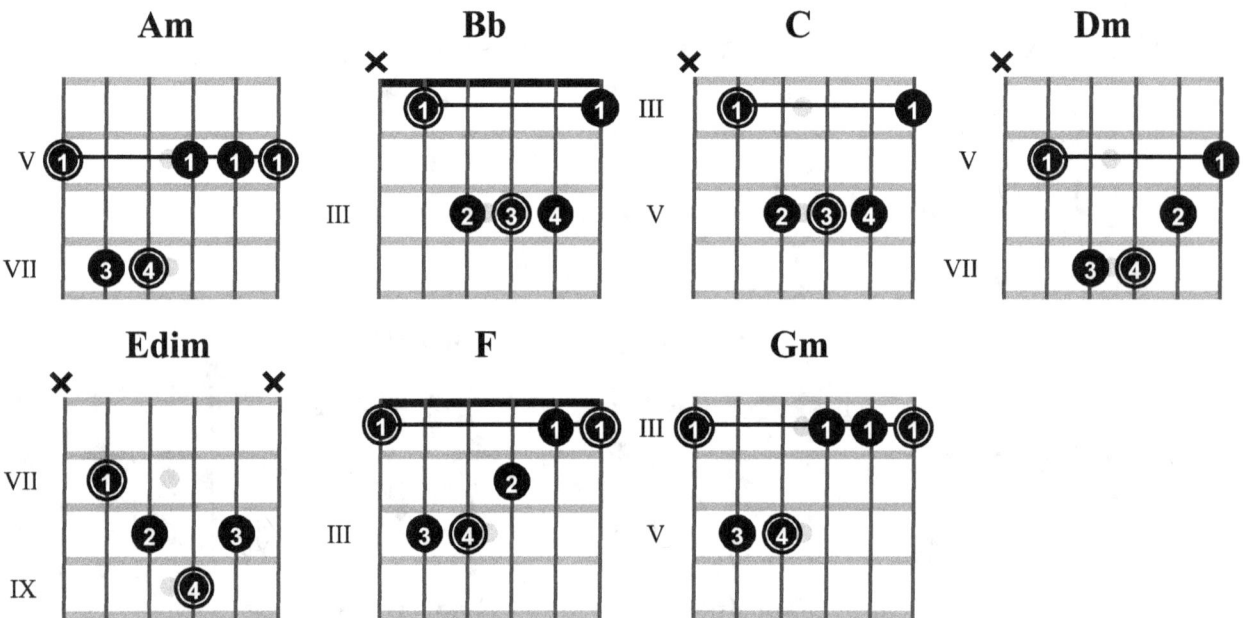

7th Chords:

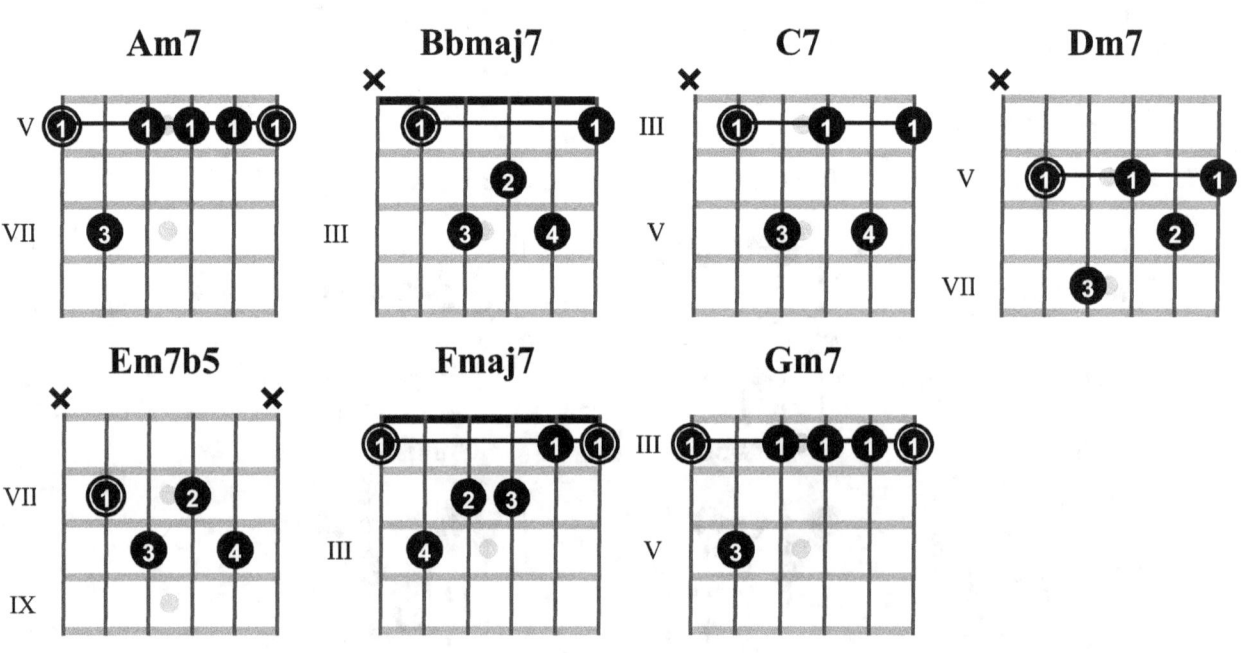

A Phrygian Scale
continued

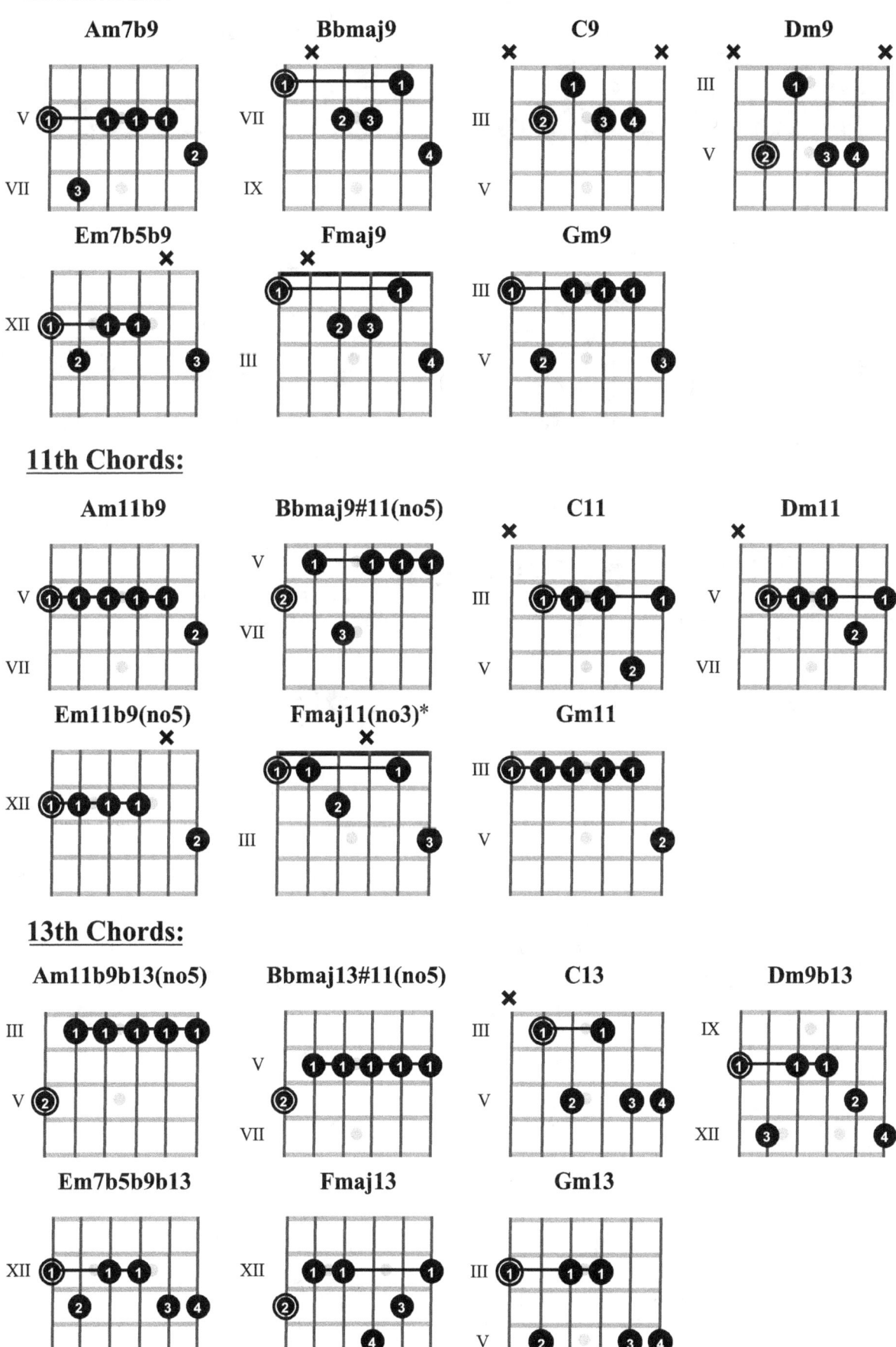

9th Chords:

Am7b9   Bbmaj9   C9   Dm9

Em7b5b9   Fmaj9   Gm9

11th Chords:

Am11b9   Bbmaj9#11(no5)   C11   Dm11

Em11b9(no5)   Fmaj11(no3)*   Gm11

13th Chords:

Am11b9b13(no5)   Bbmaj13#11(no5)   C13   Dm9b13

Em7b5b9b13   Fmaj13   Gm13

A Lydian Scale

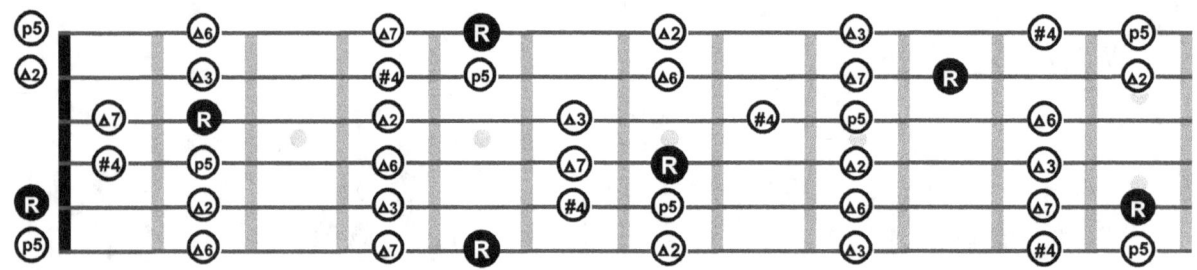

Triad Chords:

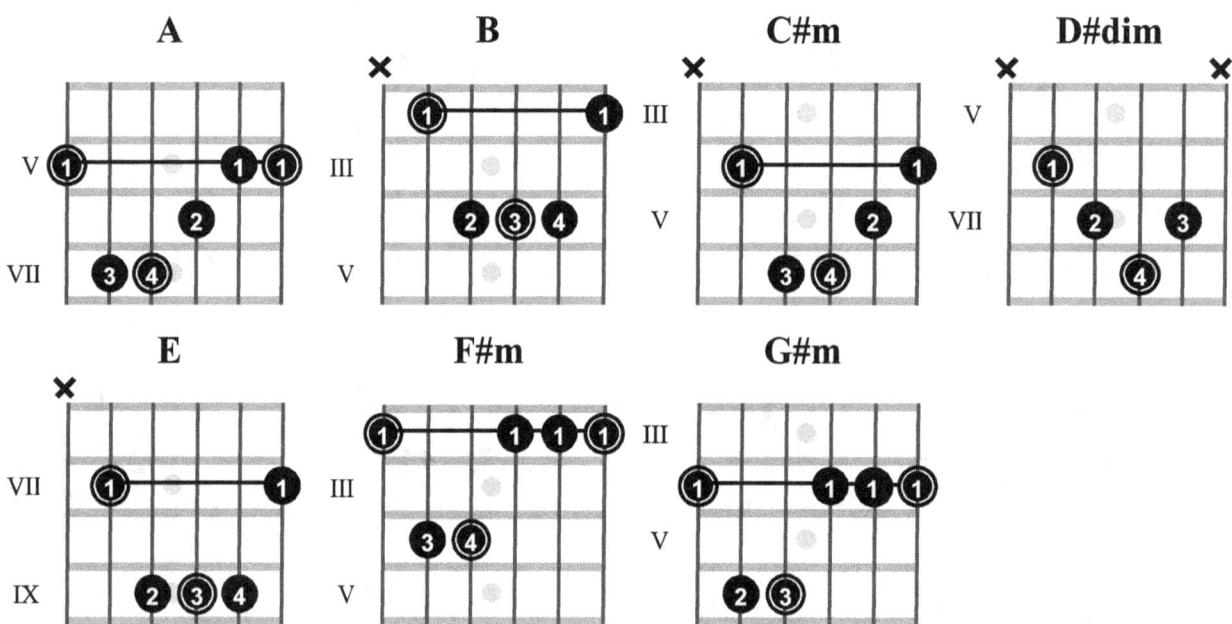

7th Chords:

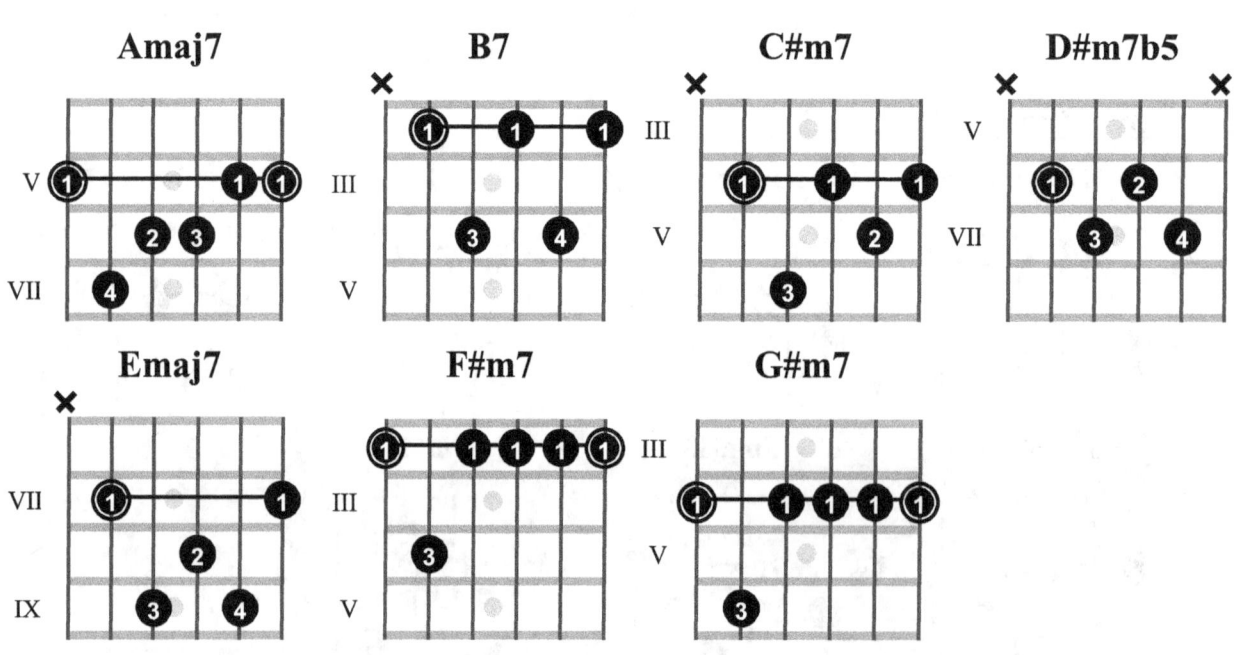

A Lydian Scale
continued

9th Chords:

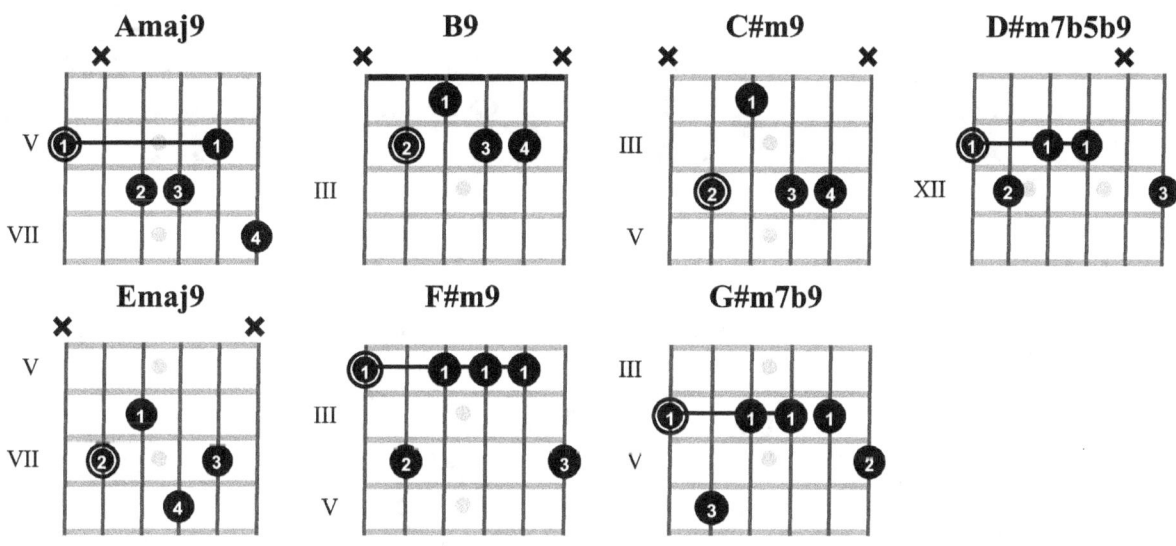

Amaj9 B9 C#m9 D#m7b5b9

Emaj9 F#m9 G#m7b9

11th Chords:

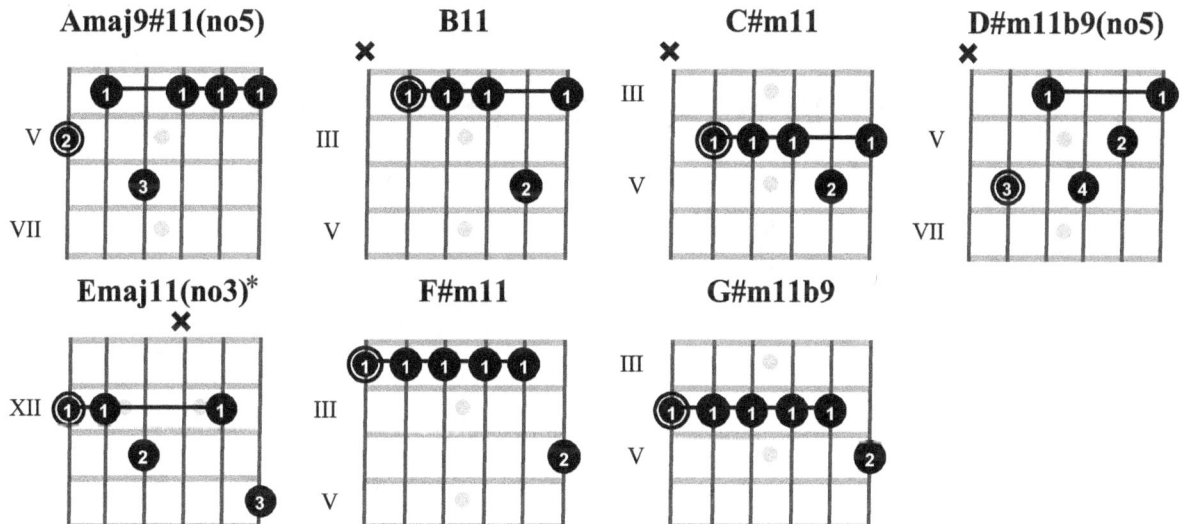

Amaj9#11(no5) B11 C#m11 D#m11b9(no5)

Emaj11(no3)* F#m11 G#m11b9

13th Chords:

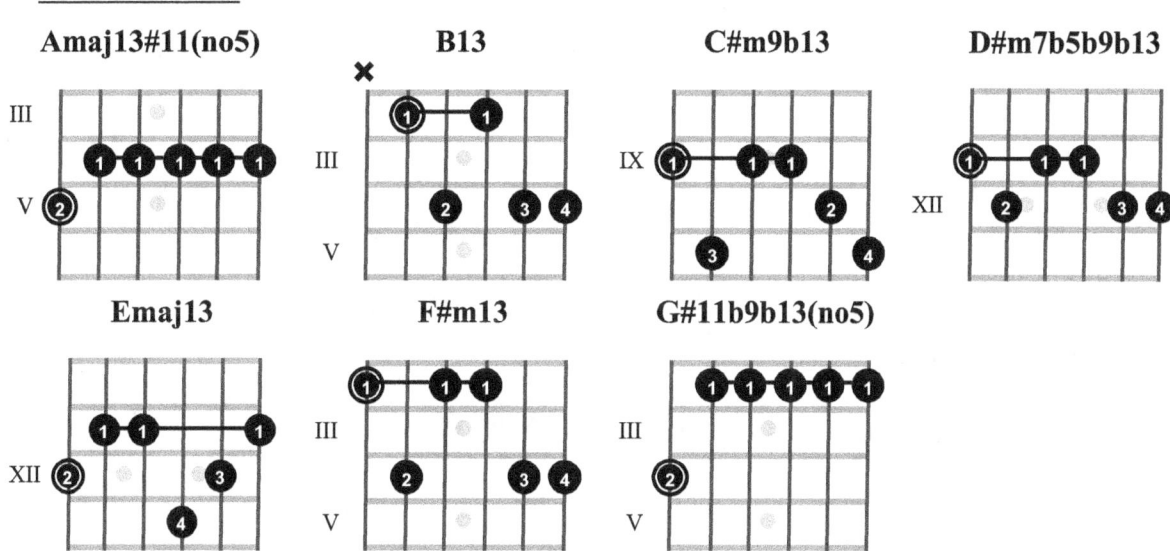

Amaj13#11(no5) B13 C#m9b13 D#m7b5b9b13

Emaj13 F#m13 G#11b9b13(no5)

20

A Mixolydian Scale

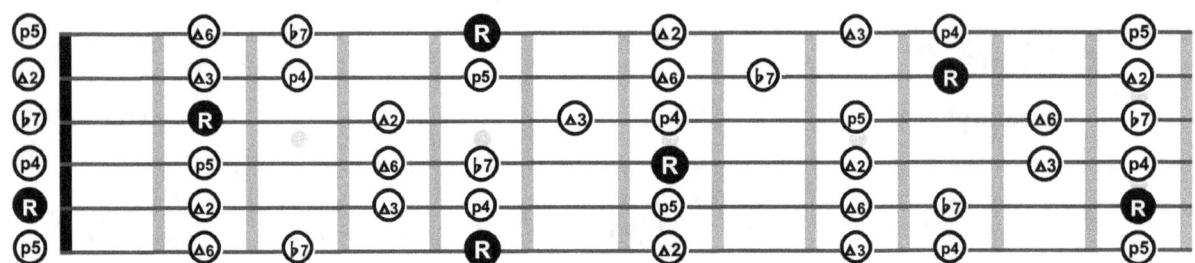

Triad Chords:

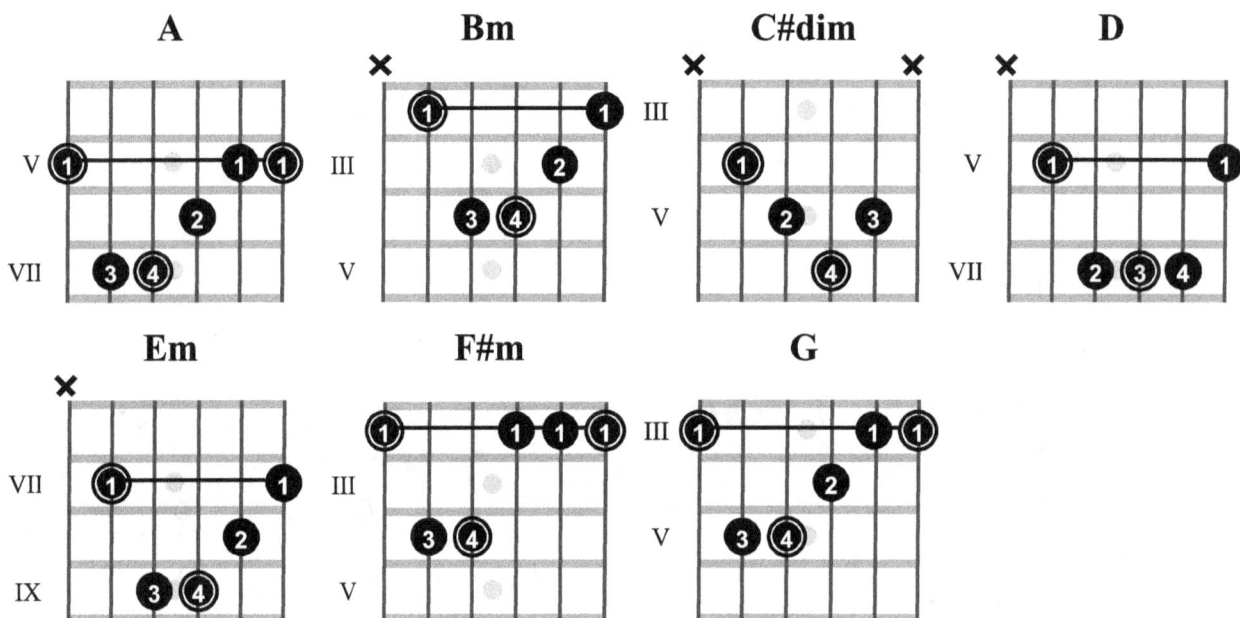

7th Chords:

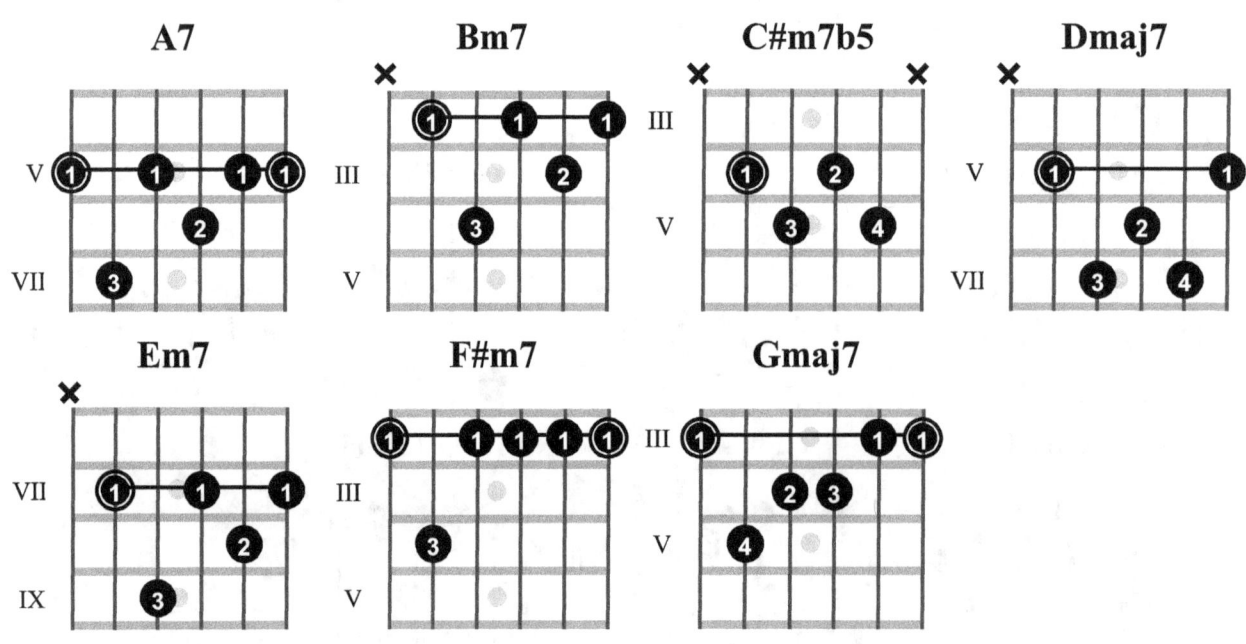

A Mixolydian Scale
continued

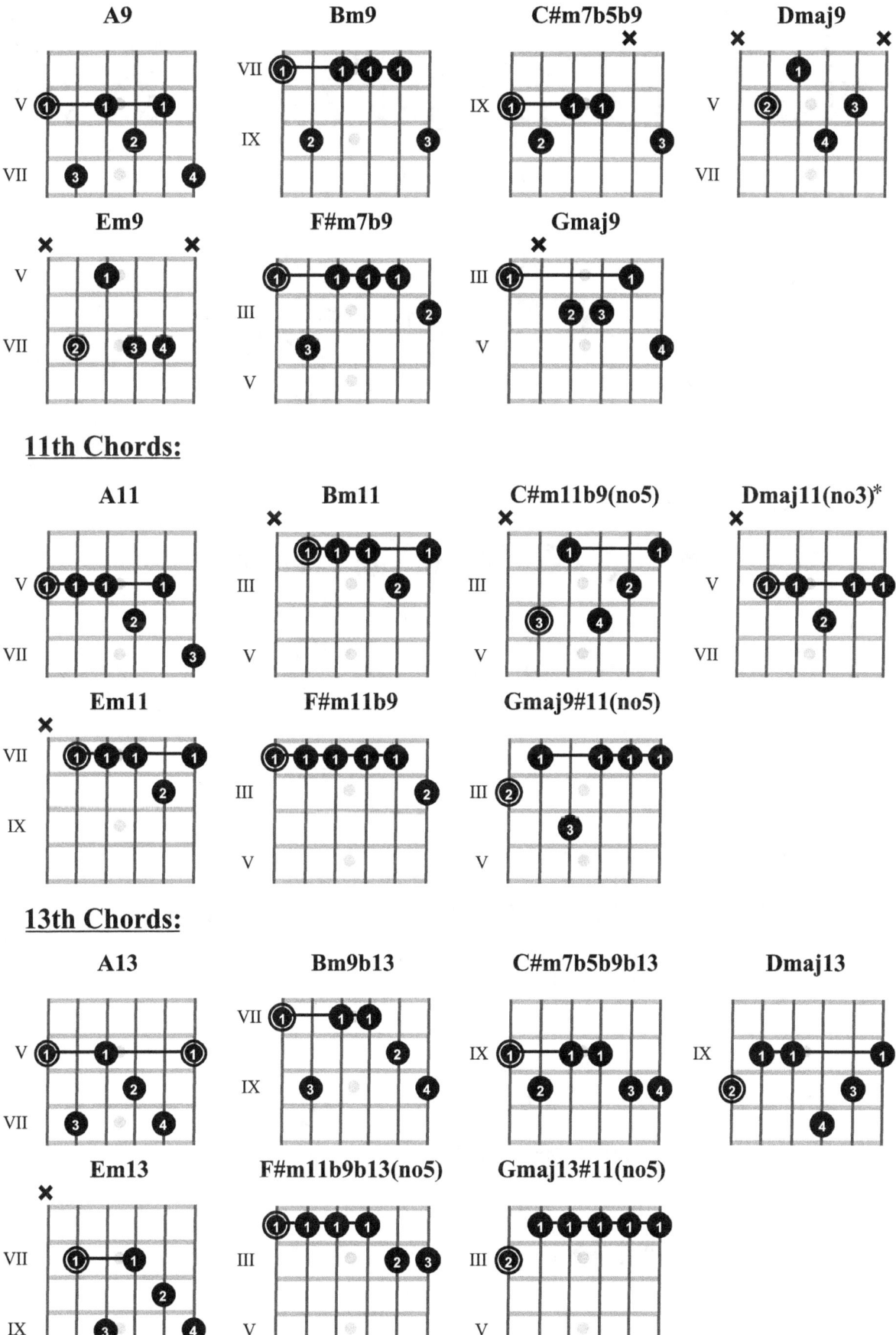

9th Chords:

A9   Bm9   C#m7b5b9   Dmaj9

Em9   F#m7b9   Gmaj9

11th Chords:

A11   Bm11   C#m11b9(no5)   Dmaj11(no3)*

Em11   F#m11b9   Gmaj9#11(no5)

13th Chords:

A13   Bm9b13   C#m7b5b9b13   Dmaj13

Em13   F#m11b9b13(no5)   Gmaj13#11(no5)

A Locrian Scale

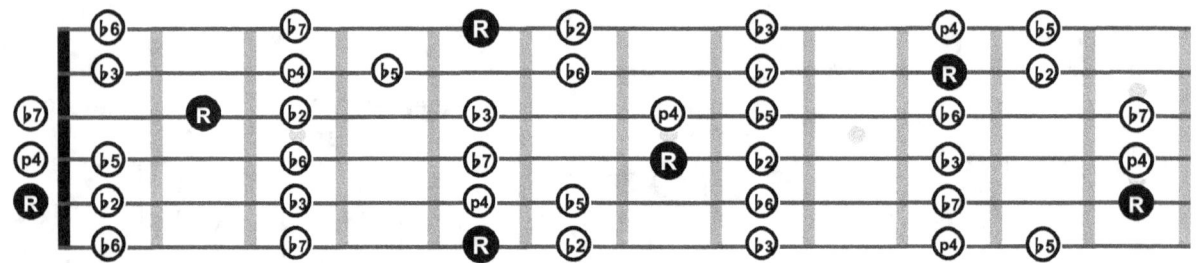

Triad Chords:

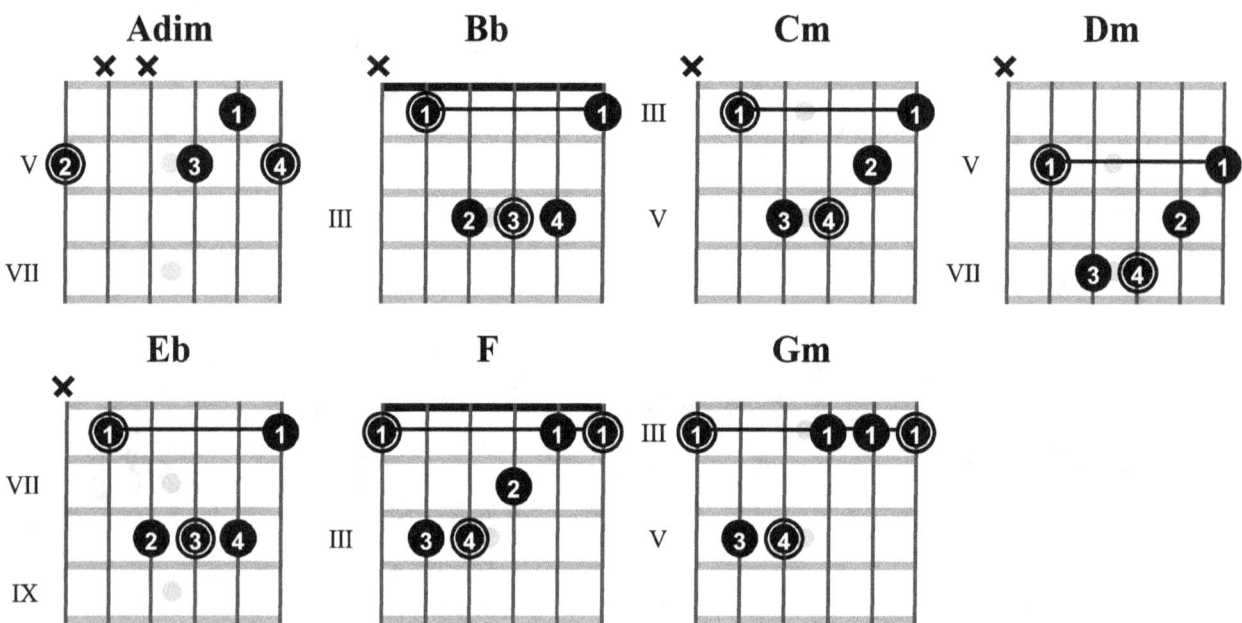

7th Chords:

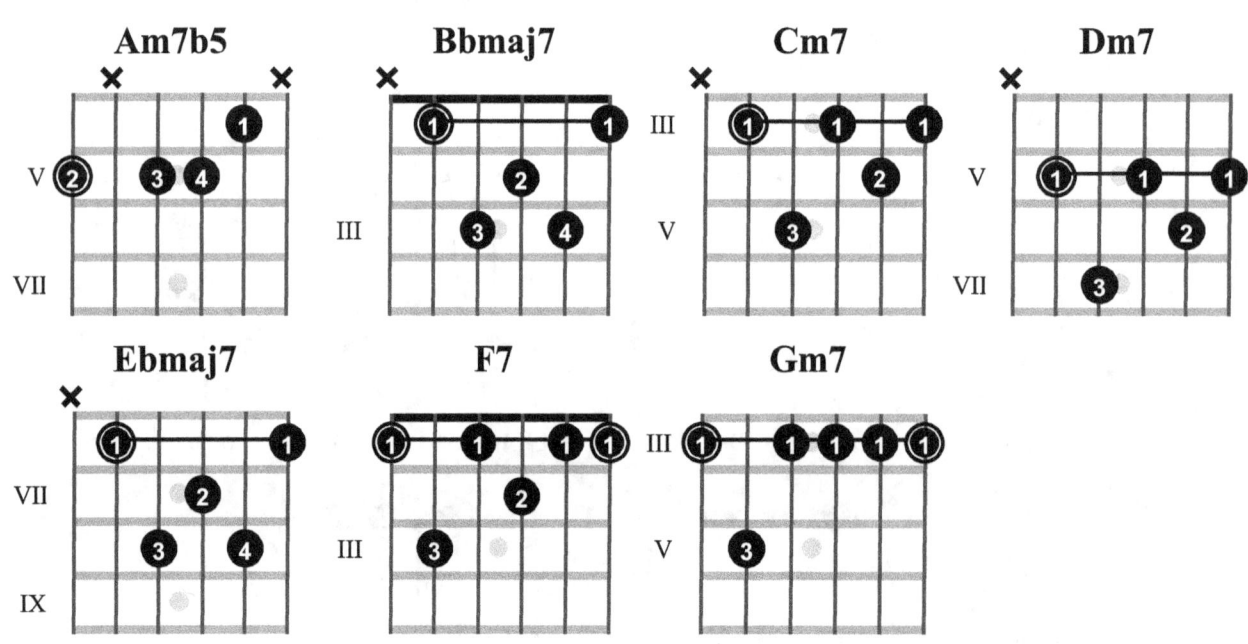

A Locrian Scale
continued

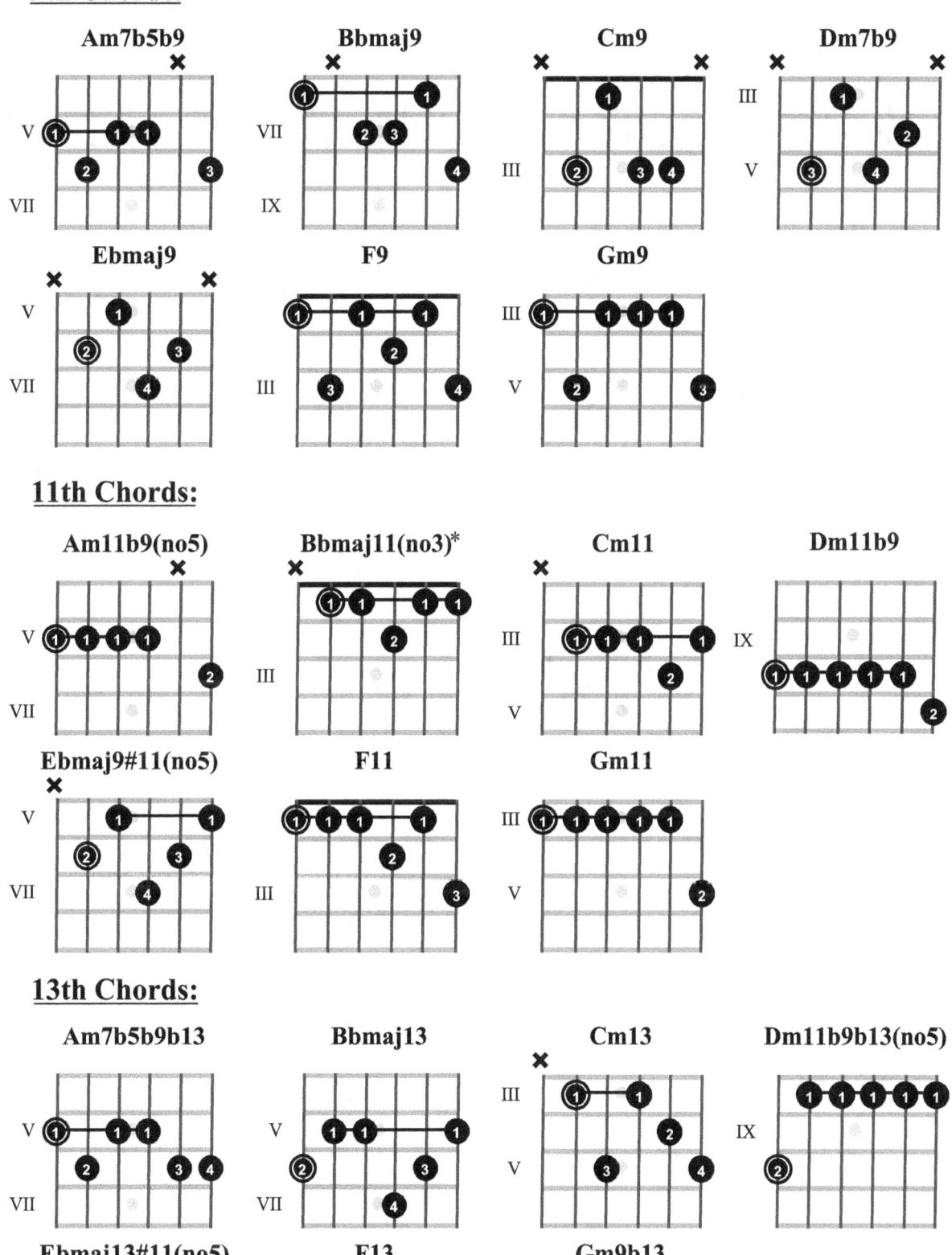

9th Chords:

Am7b5b9   Bbmaj9   Cm9   Dm7b9

Ebmaj9   F9   Gm9

11th Chords:

Am11b9(no5)   Bbmaj11(no3)*   Cm11   Dm11b9

Ebmaj9#11(no5)   F11   Gm11

13th Chords:

Am7b5b9b13   Bbmaj13   Cm13   Dm11b9b13(no5)

Ebmaj13#11(no5)   F13   Gm9b13

A Harmonic Minor Scale

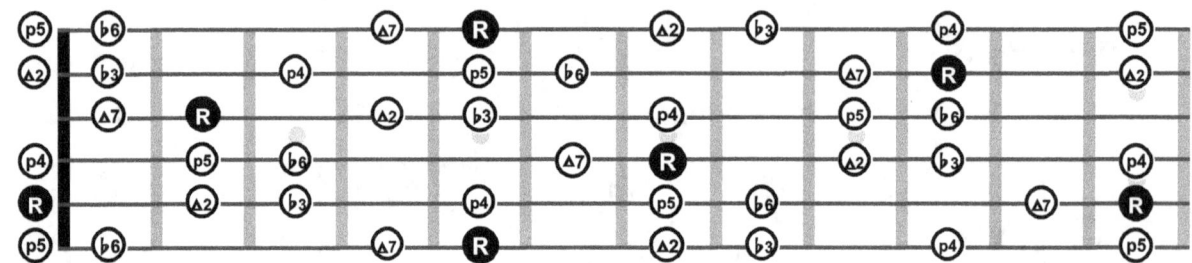

Triad Chords:

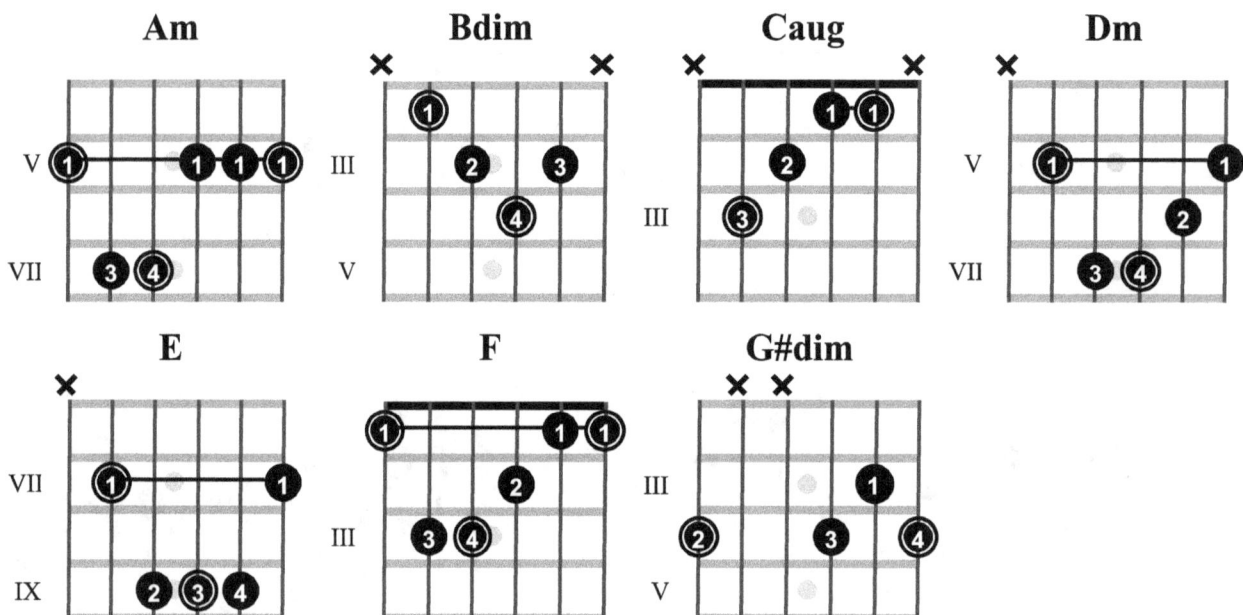

Am   Bdim   Caug   Dm

E   F   G#dim

7th Chords:

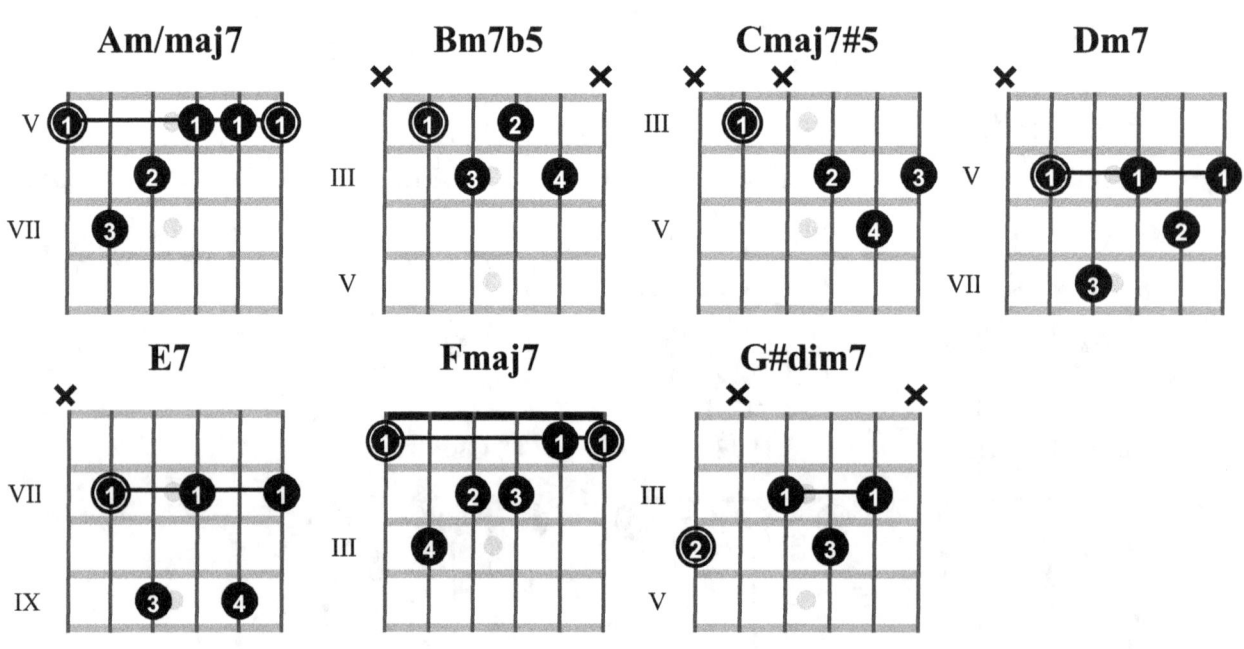

Am/maj7   Bm7b5   Cmaj7#5   Dm7

E7   Fmaj7   G#dim7

A Harmonic Minor Scale
continued

9th Chords:

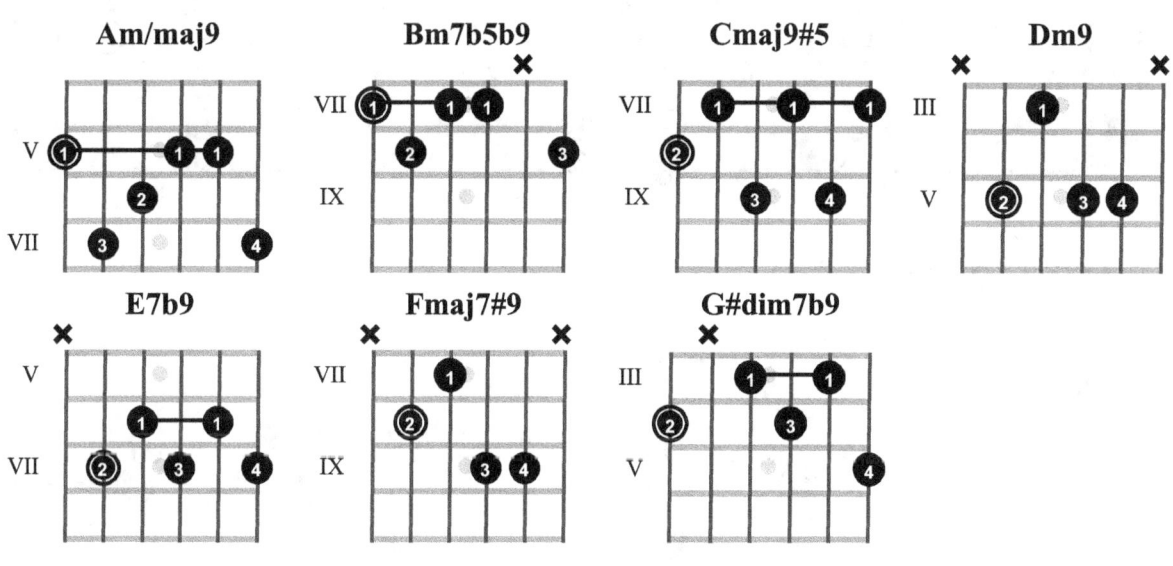

11th Chords:

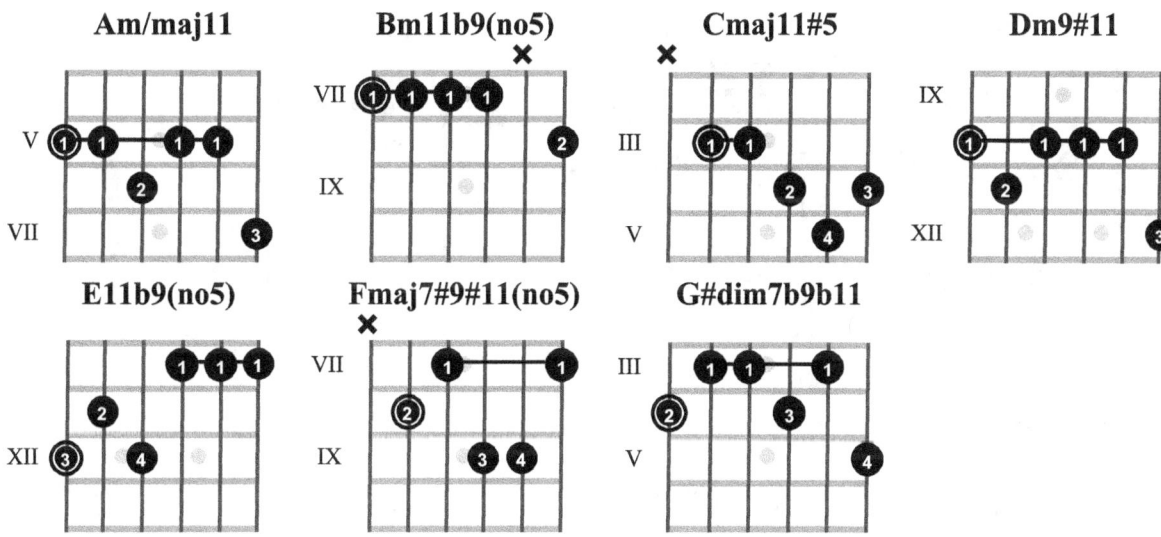

13th Chords:

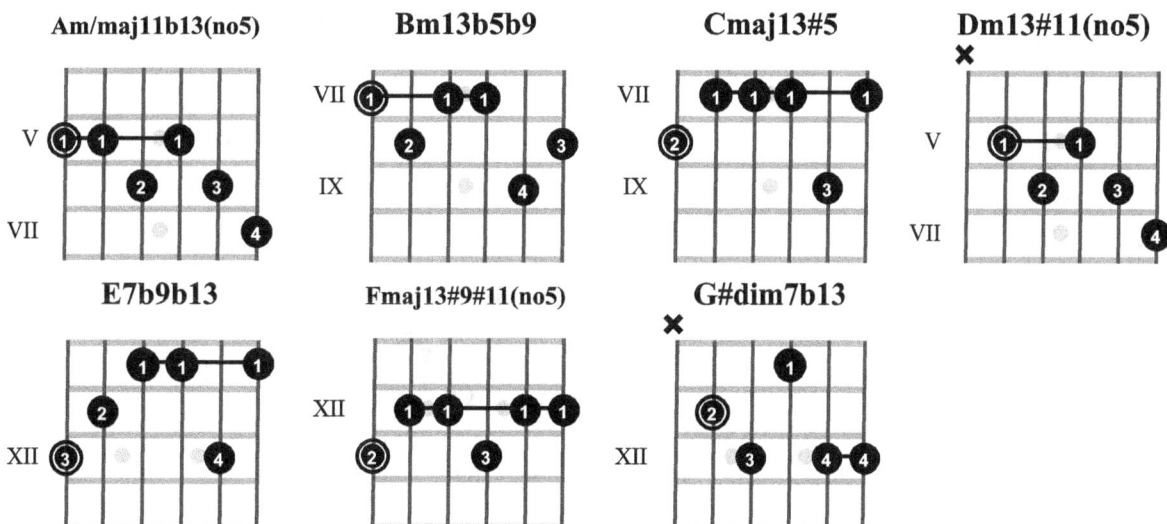

A Locrian #6 Scale

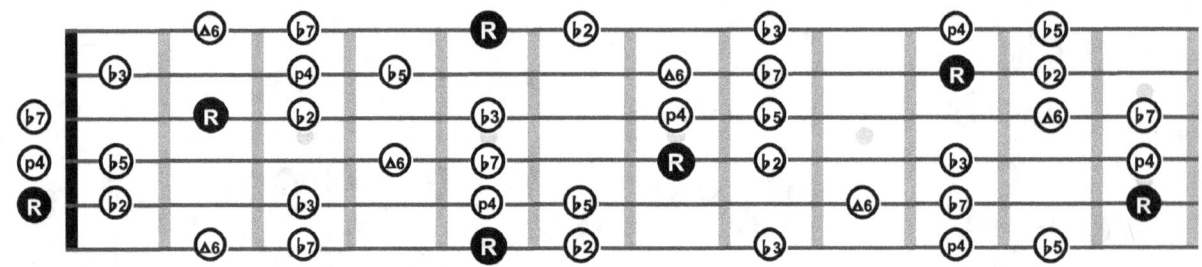

Triad Chords:

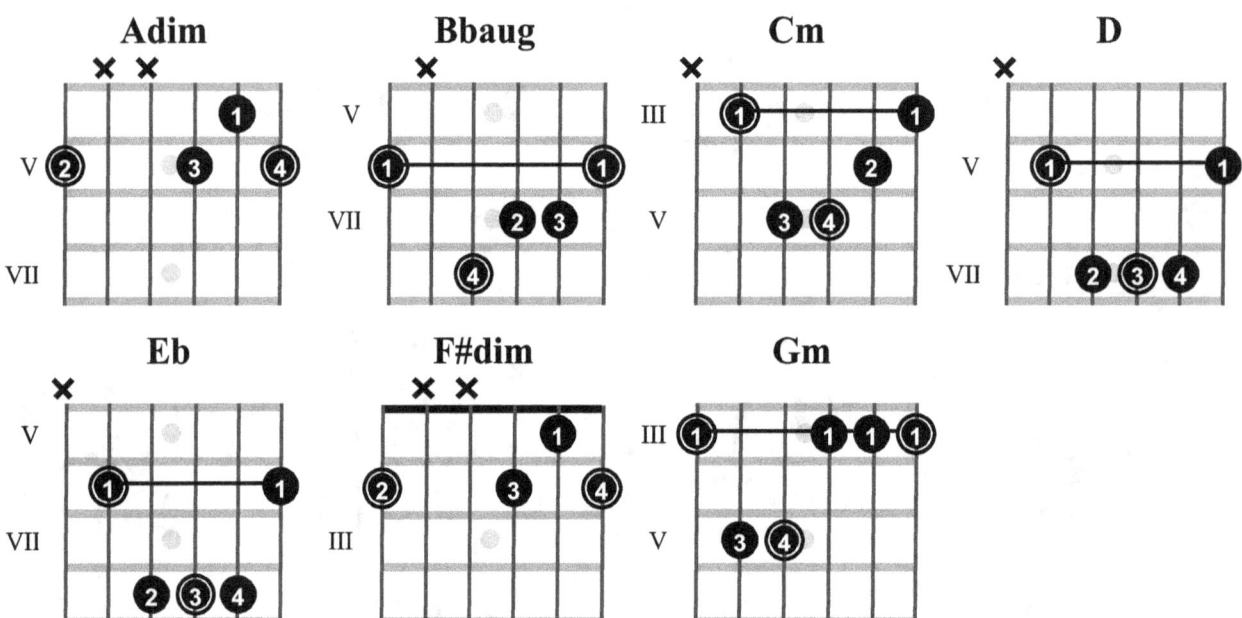

7th Chords:

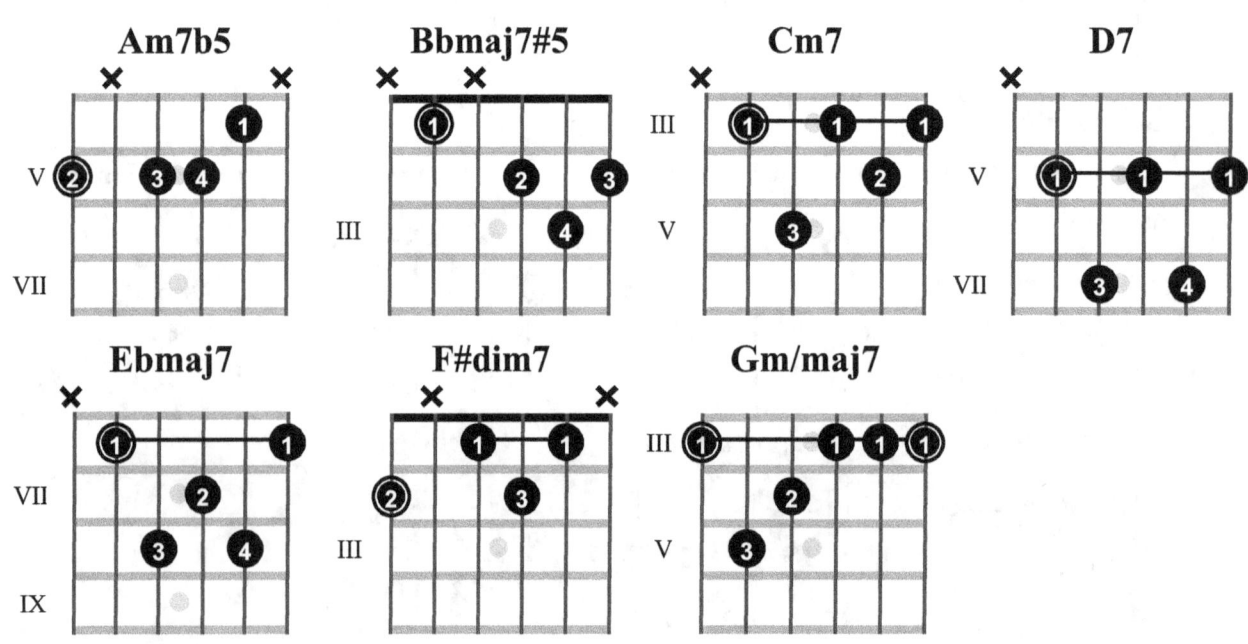

A Locrian #6 Scale
continued

9th Chords:

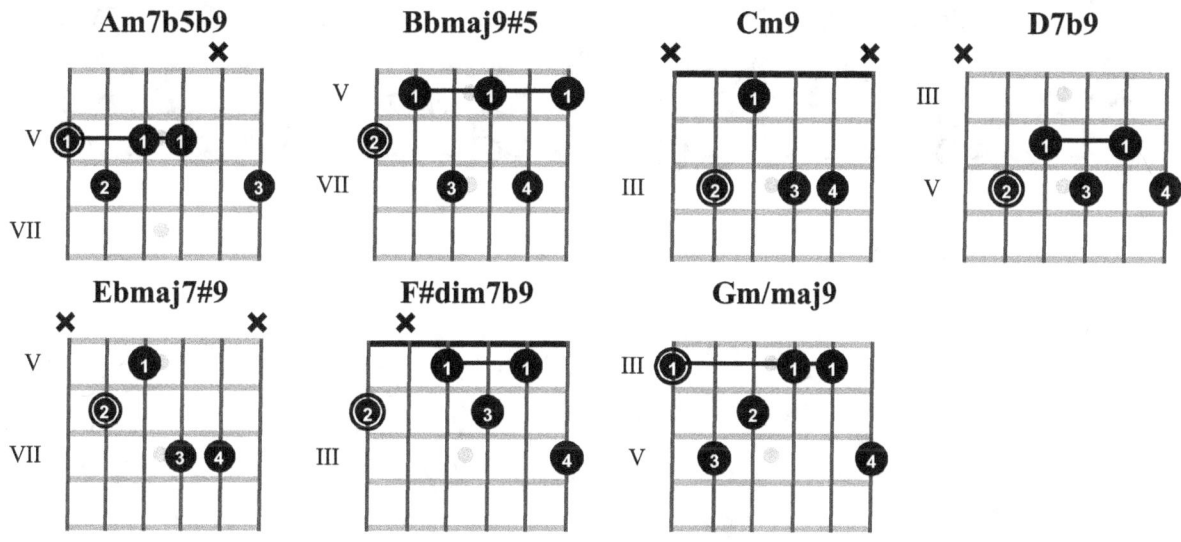

Am7b5b9   Bbmaj9#5   Cm9   D7b9

Ebmaj7#9   F#dim7b9   Gm/maj9

11th Chords:

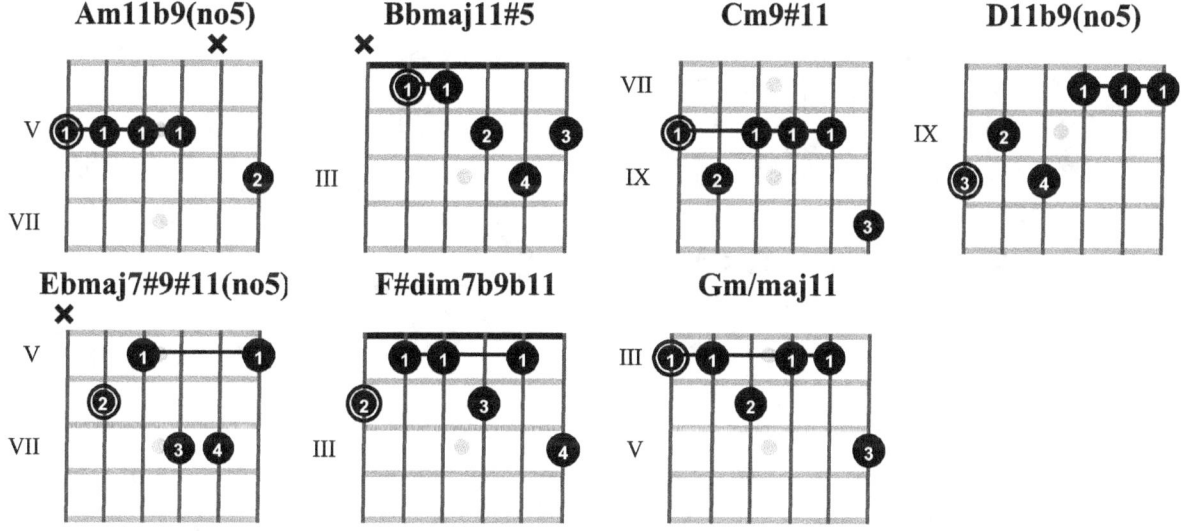

Am11b9(no5)   Bbmaj11#5   Cm9#11   D11b9(no5)

Ebmaj7#9#11(no5)   F#dim7b9b11   Gm/maj11

13th Chords:

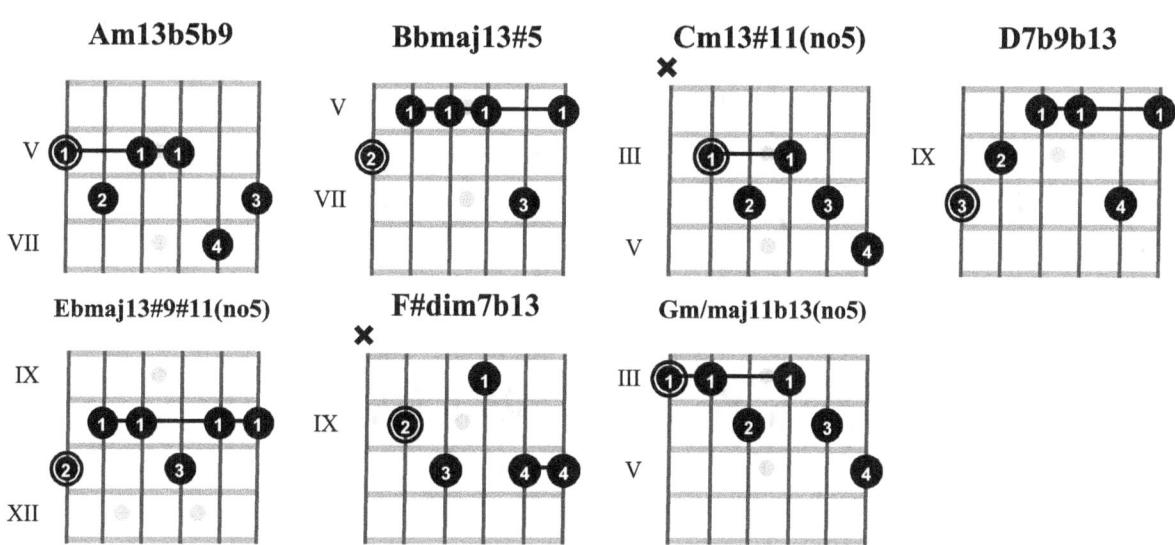

Am13b5b9   Bbmaj13#5   Cm13#11(no5)   D7b9b13

Ebmaj13#9#11(no5)   F#dim7b13   Gm/maj11b13(no5)

A Ionian Augmented Scale

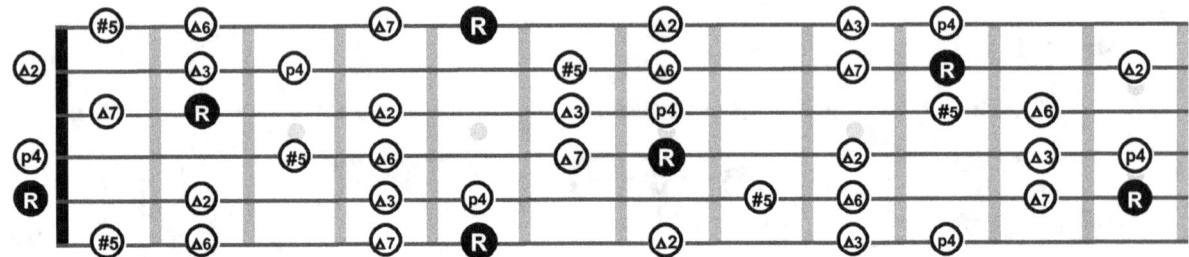

Triad Chords:

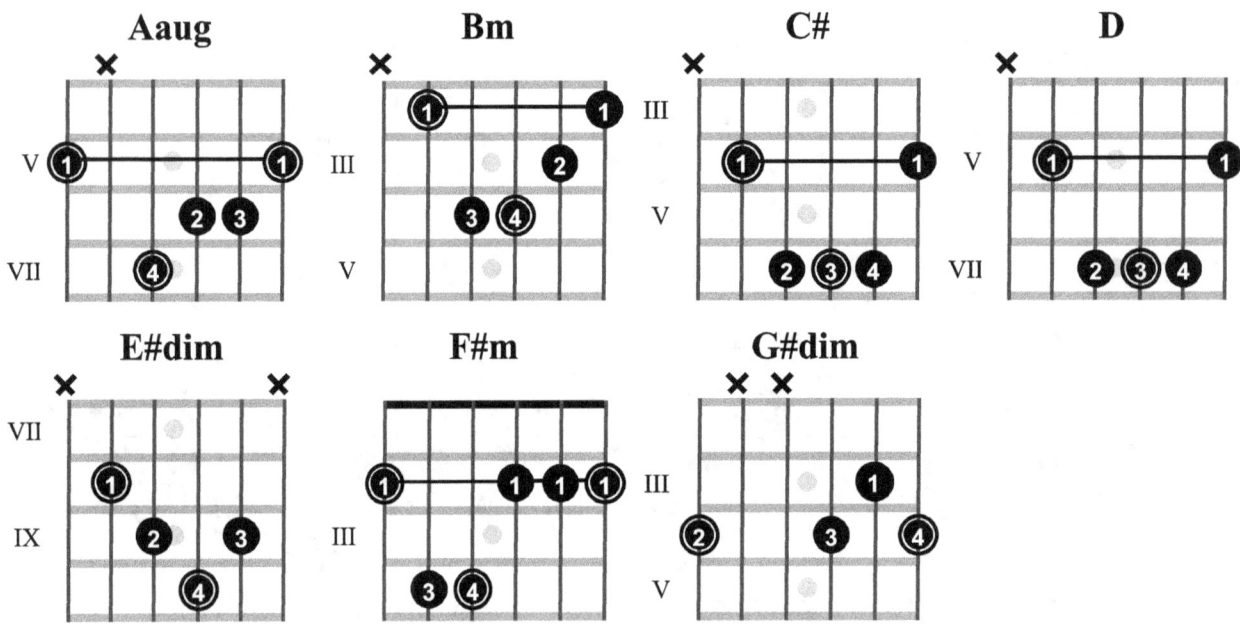

7th Chords:

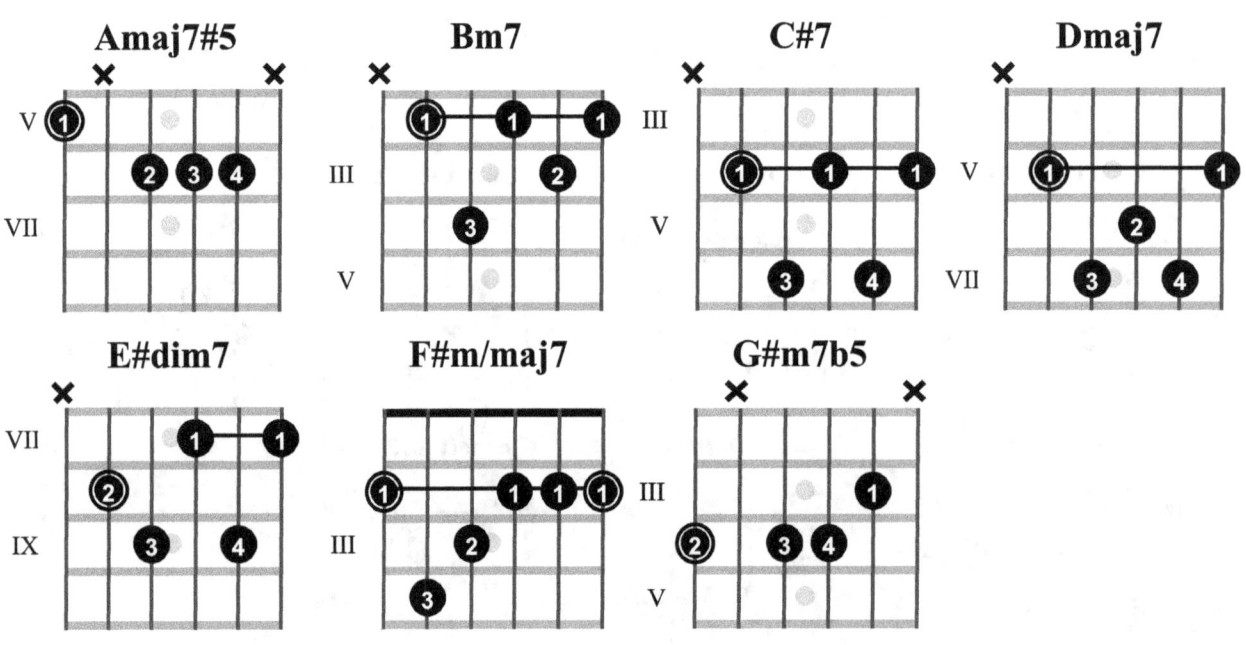

A Ionian Augmented Scale
continued

9th Chords:

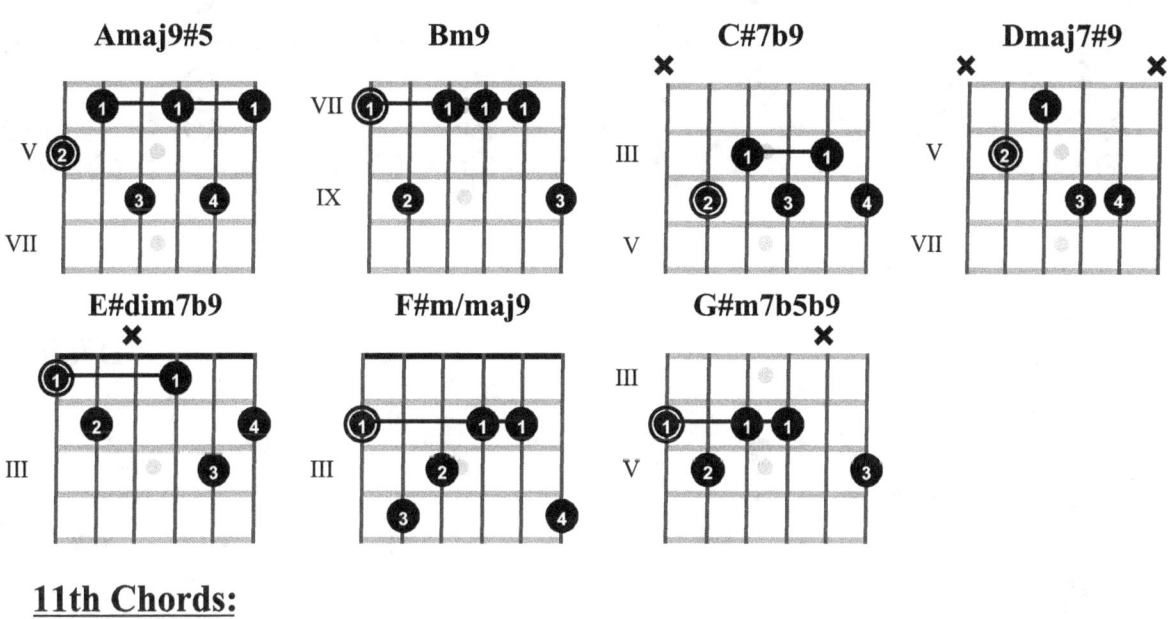

Amaj9#5   Bm9   C#7b9   Dmaj7#9

E#dim7b9   F#m/maj9   G#m7b5b9

11th Chords:

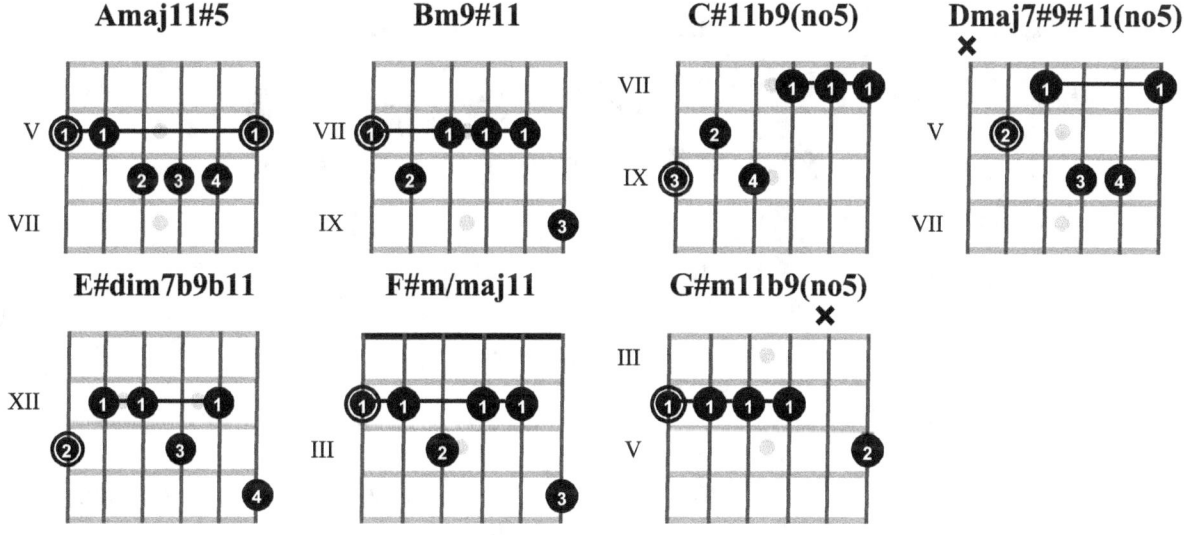

Amaj11#5   Bm9#11   C#11b9(no5)   Dmaj7#9#11(no5)

E#dim7b9b11   F#m/maj11   G#m11b9(no5)

13th Chords:

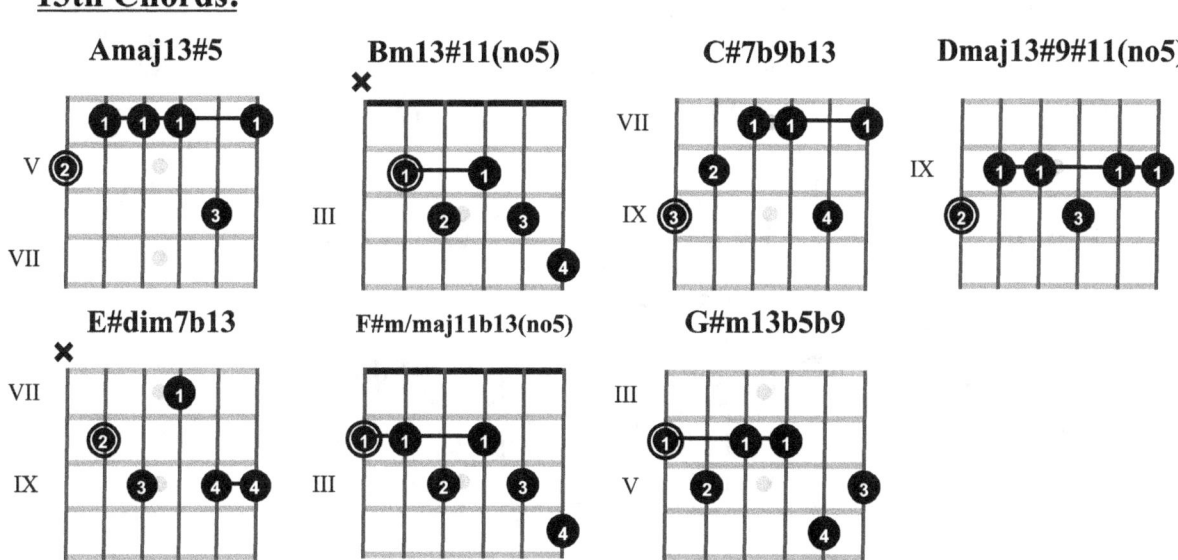

Amaj13#5   Bm13#11(no5)   C#7b9b13   Dmaj13#9#11(no5)

E#dim7b13   F#m/maj11b13(no5)   G#m13b5b9

A Dorian #4 Scale

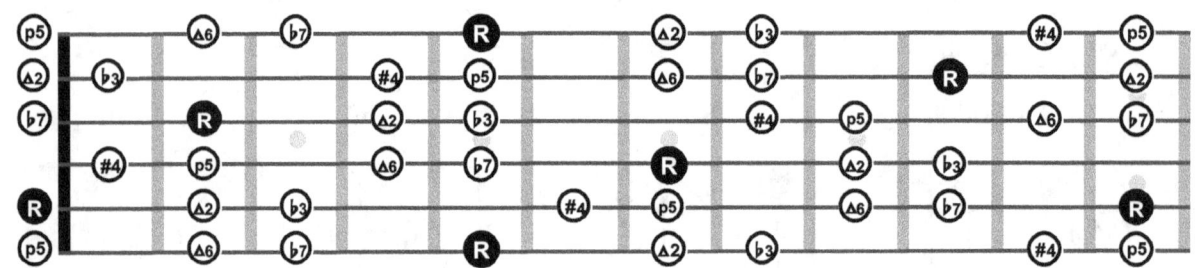

Triad Chords:

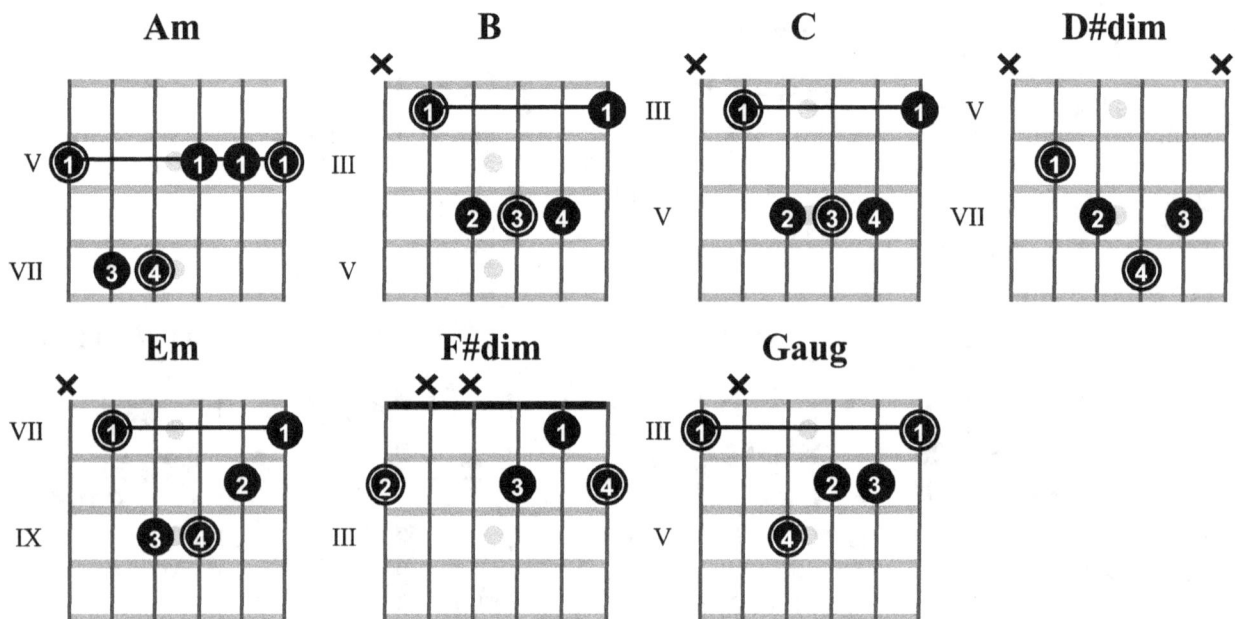

7th Chords:

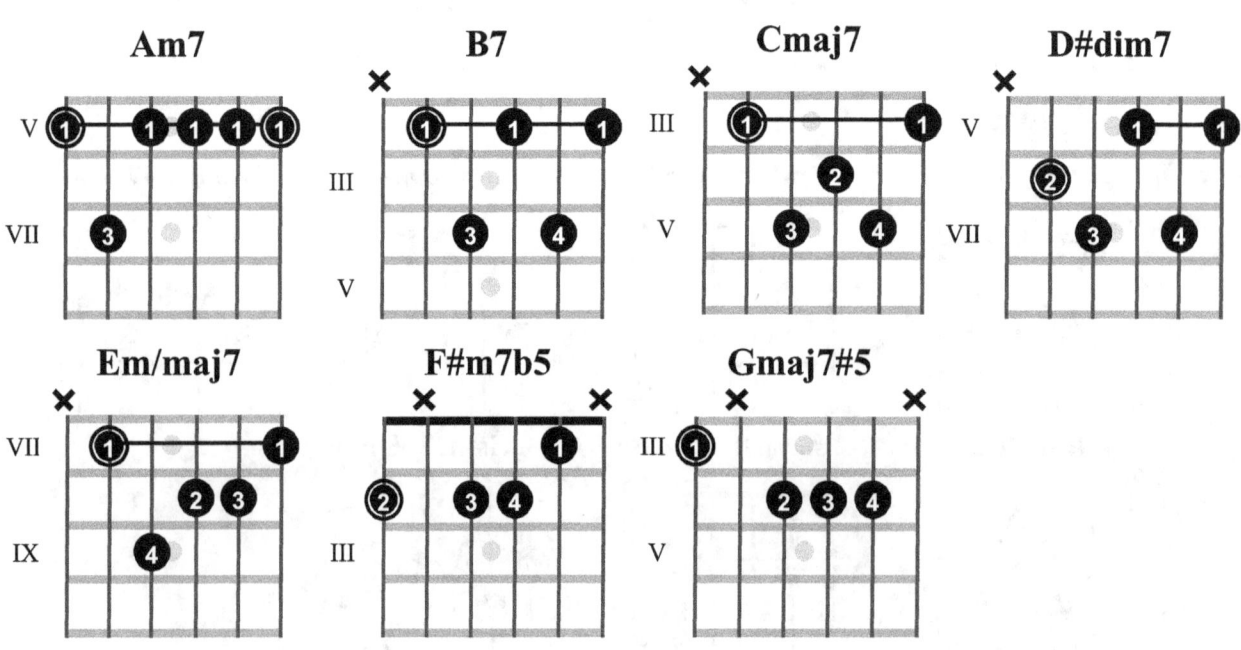

A Dorian #4 Scale
continued

9th Chords:

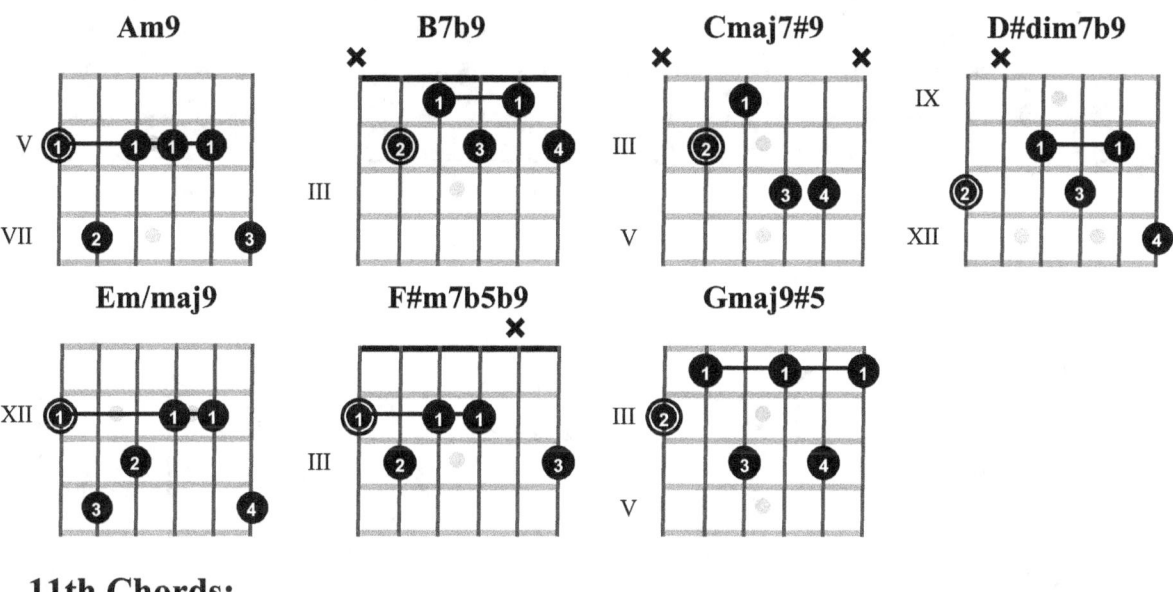

Am9   B7b9   Cmaj7#9   D#dim7b9

Em/maj9   F#m7b5b9   Gmaj9#5

11th Chords:

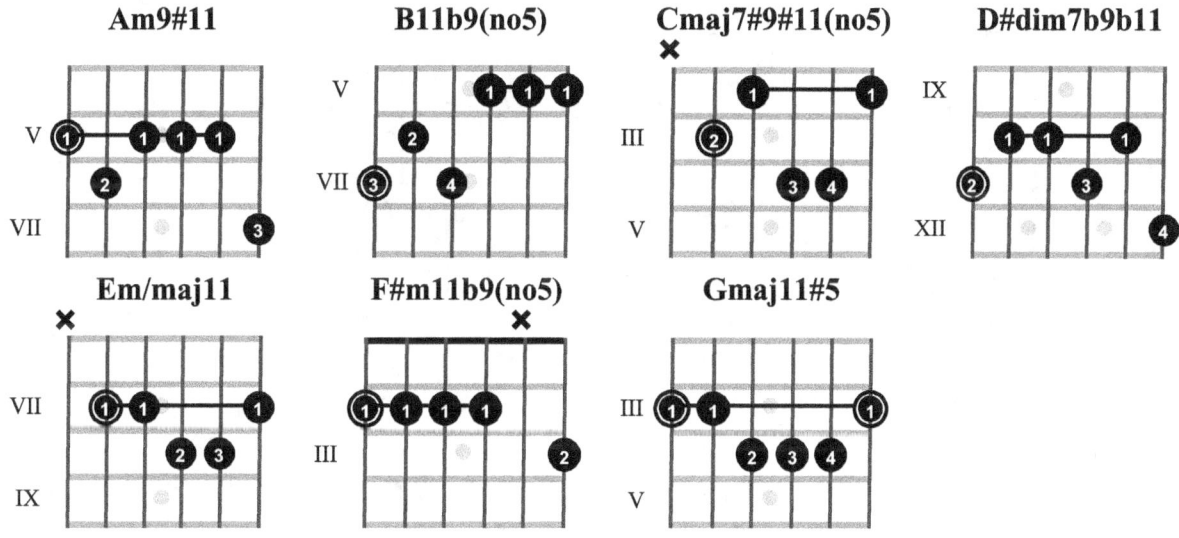

Am9#11   B11b9(no5)   Cmaj7#9#11(no5)   D#dim7b9b11

Em/maj11   F#m11b9(no5)   Gmaj11#5

13th Chords:

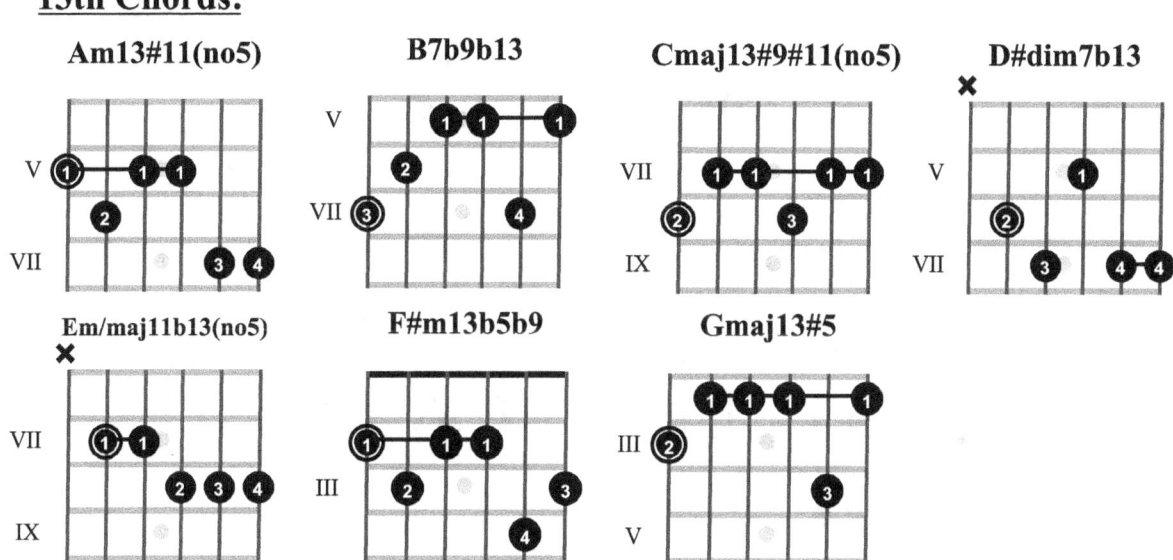

Am13#11(no5)   B7b9b13   Cmaj13#9#11(no5)   D#dim7b13

Em/maj11b13(no5)   F#m13b5b9   Gmaj13#5

A Phrygian Dominant Scale

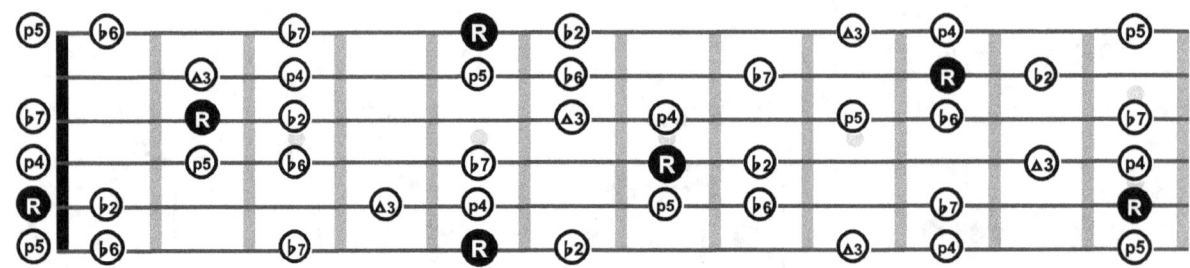

Triad Chords:

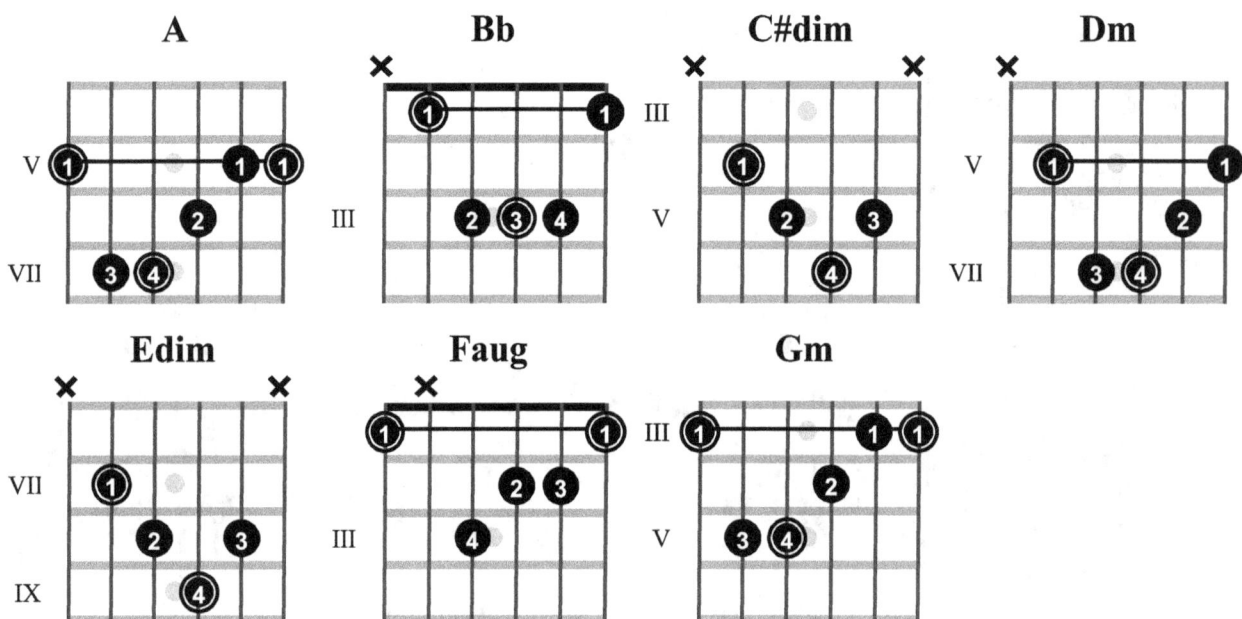

A   Bb   C#dim   Dm

Edim   Faug   Gm

7th Chords:

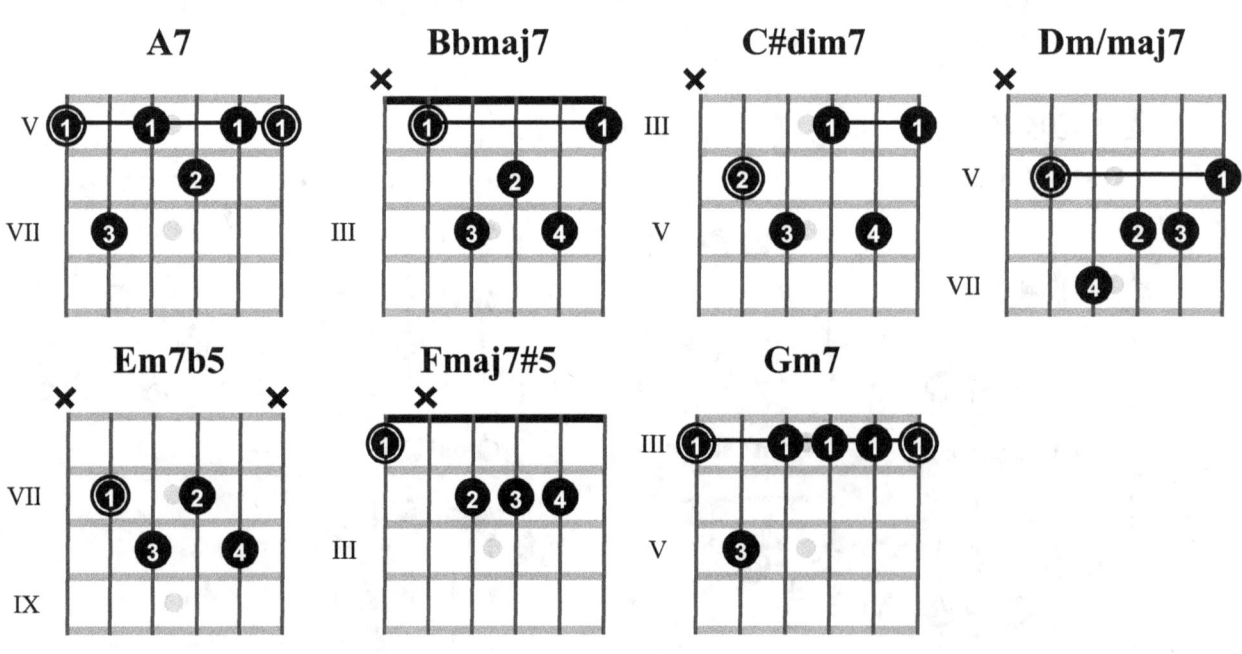

A7   Bbmaj7   C#dim7   Dm/maj7

Em7b5   Fmaj7#5   Gm7

A Phrygian Dominant Scale
continued

9th Chords:

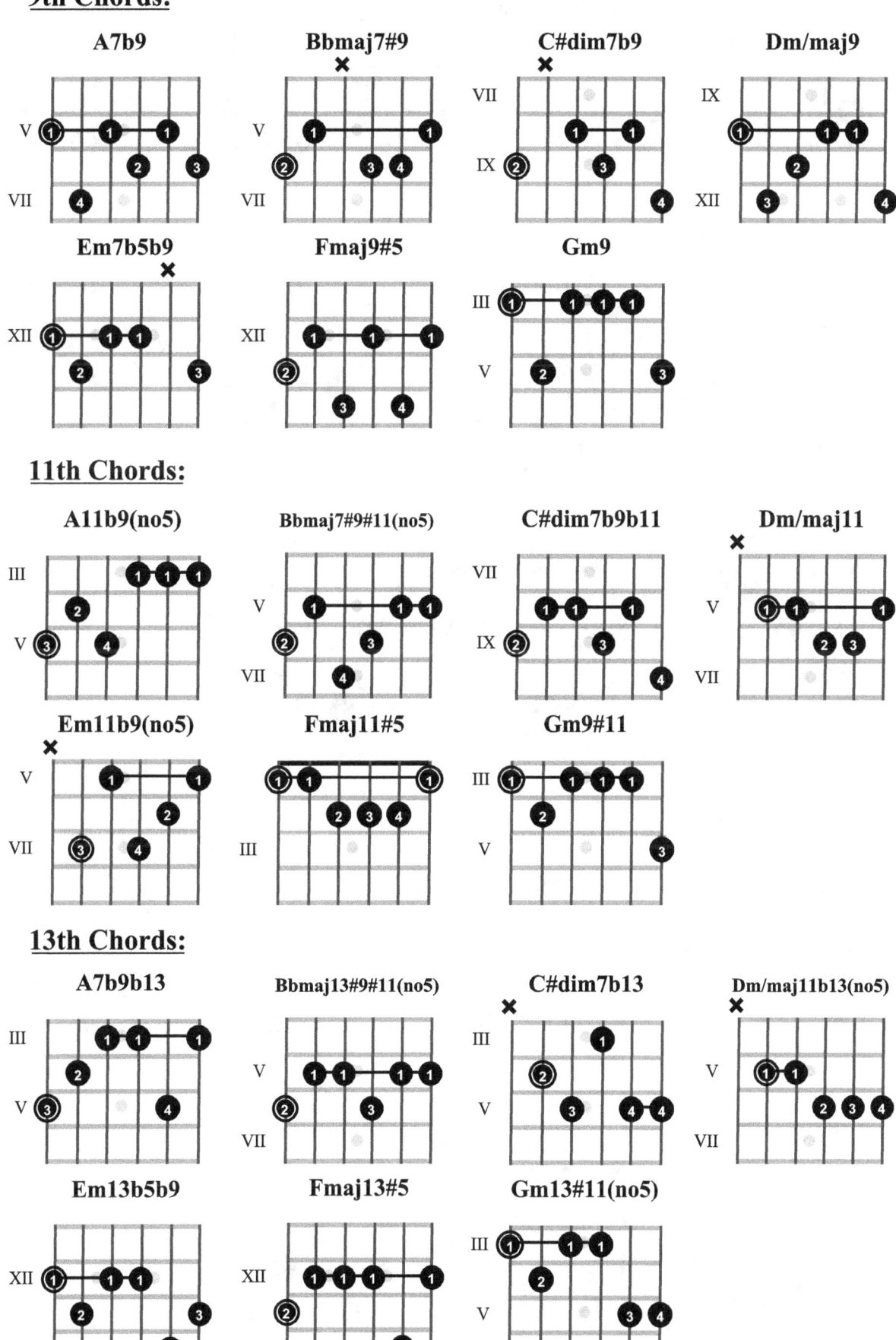

A7b9   Bbmaj7#9   C#dim7b9   Dm/maj9

Em7b5b9   Fmaj9#5   Gm9

11th Chords:

A11b9(no5)   Bbmaj7#9#11(no5)   C#dim7b9b11   Dm/maj11

Em11b9(no5)   Fmaj11#5   Gm9#11

13th Chords:

A7b9b13   Bbmaj13#9#11(no5)   C#dim7b13   Dm/maj11b13(no5)

Em13b5b9   Fmaj13#5   Gm13#11(no5)

A Lydian #2 Scale

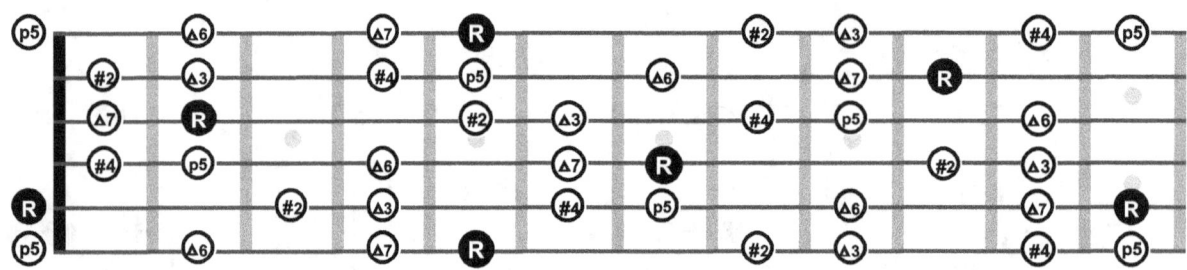

Triad Chords:

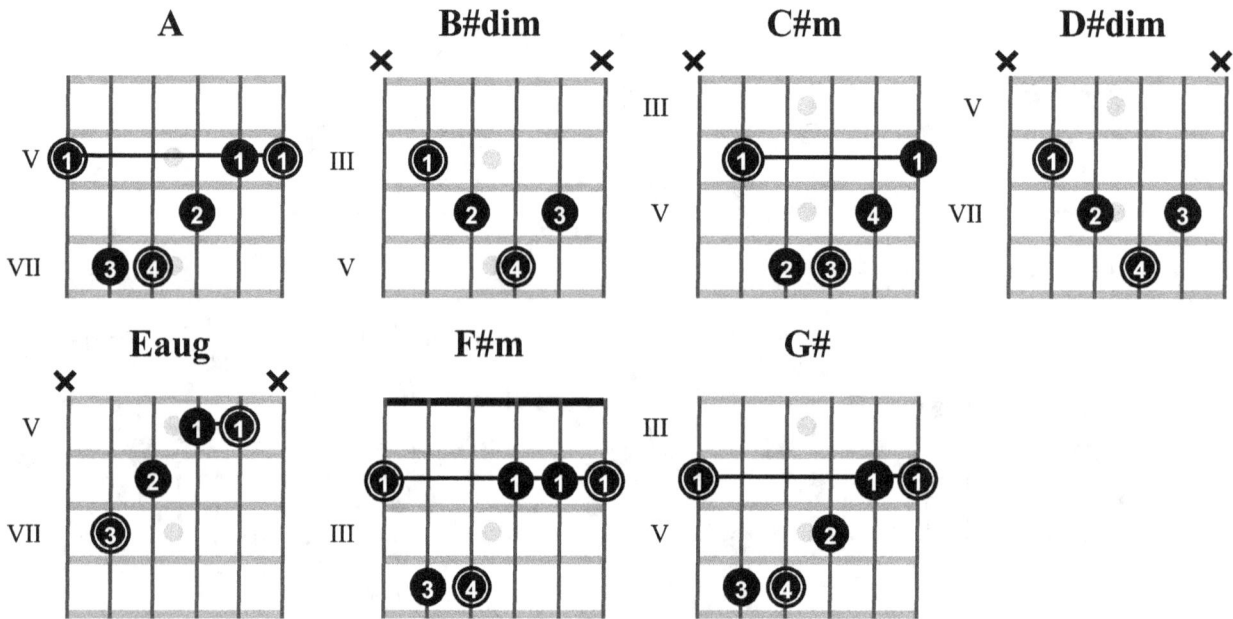

7th Chords:

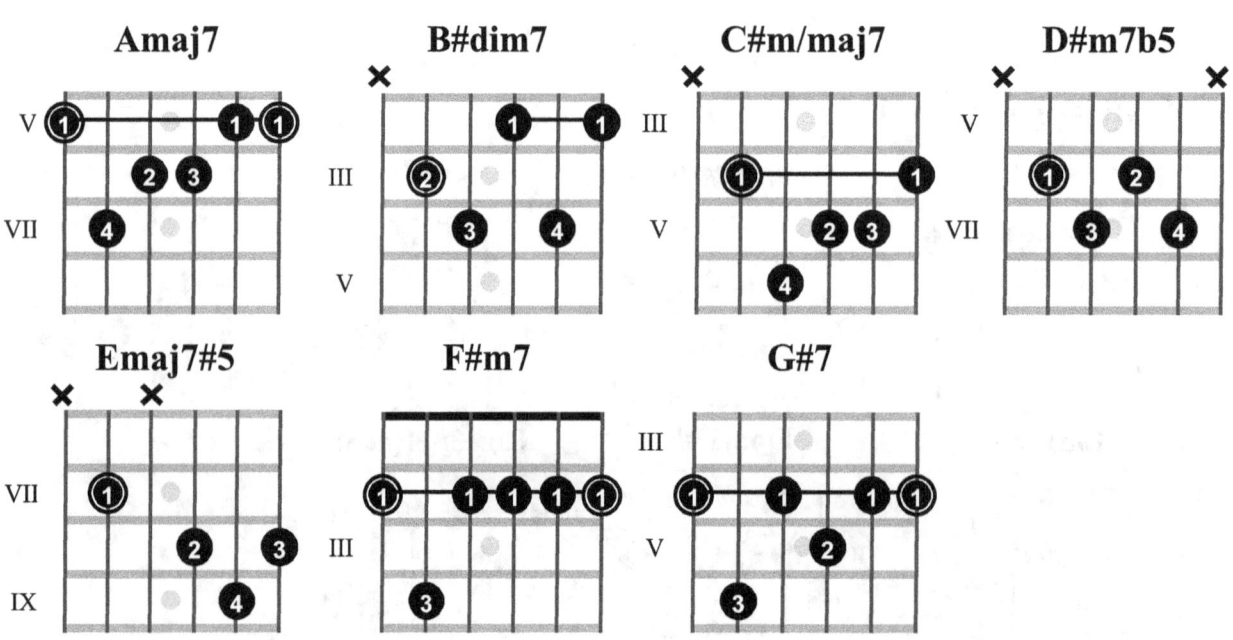

A Lydian #2 Scale
continued

9th Chords:

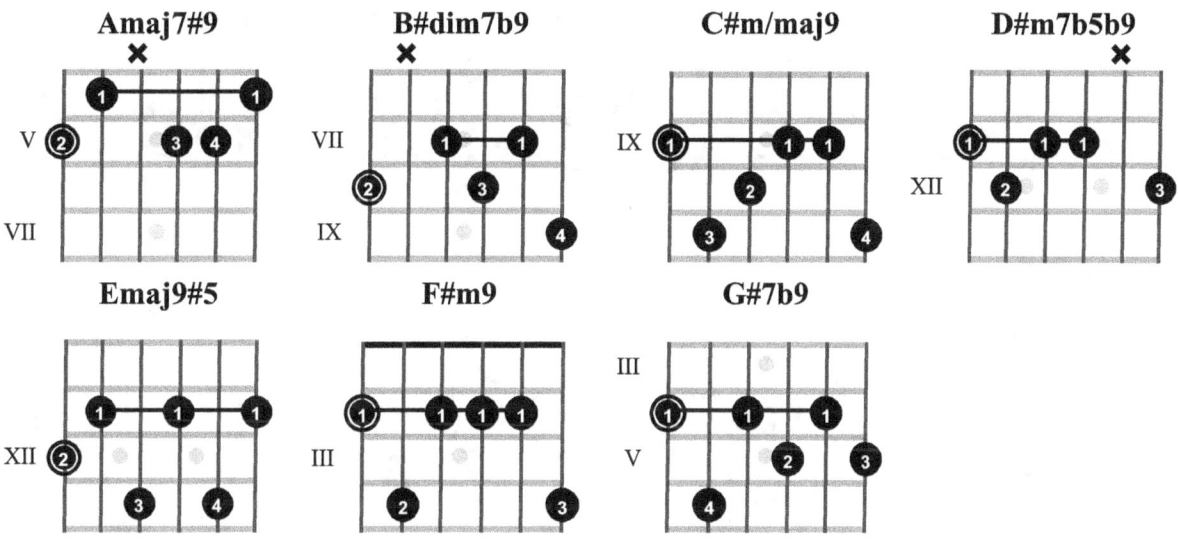

Amaj7#9   B#dim7b9   C#m/maj9   D#m7b5b9

Emaj9#5   F#m9   G#7b9

11th Chords:

Amaj7#9#11(no5)   B#dim7b9b11   C#m/maj11   D#11b9(no5)

Emaj11#5   F#m9#11   G#11b9(no5)

13th Chords:

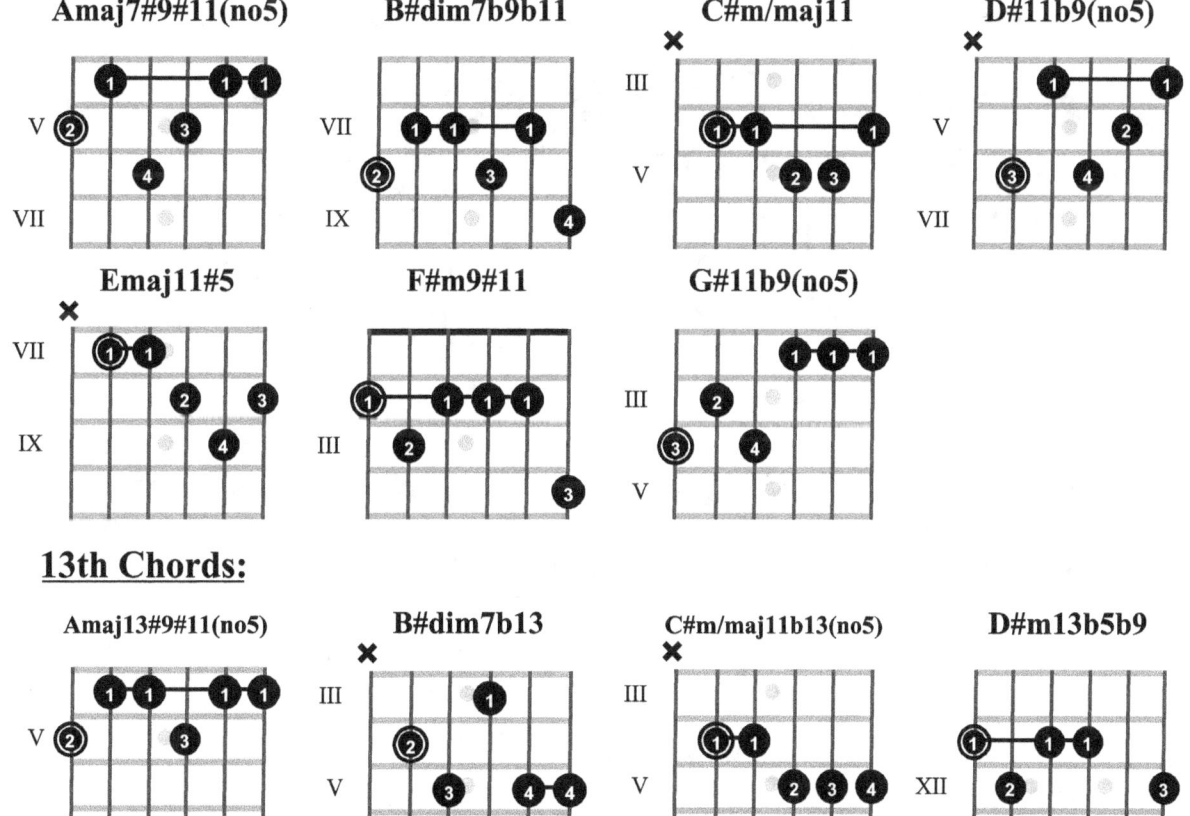

Amaj13#9#11(no5)   B#dim7b13   C#m/maj11b13(no5)   D#m13b5b9

Emaj13#5   F#m13#11(no5)   G#7b9b13

A Ultralocrian Scale

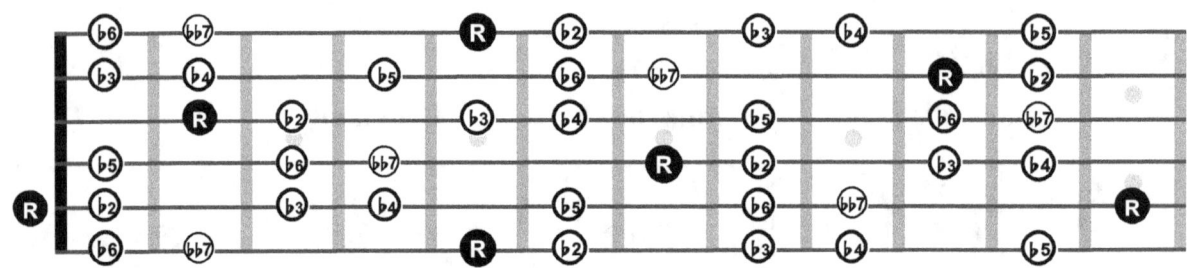

Triad Chords:

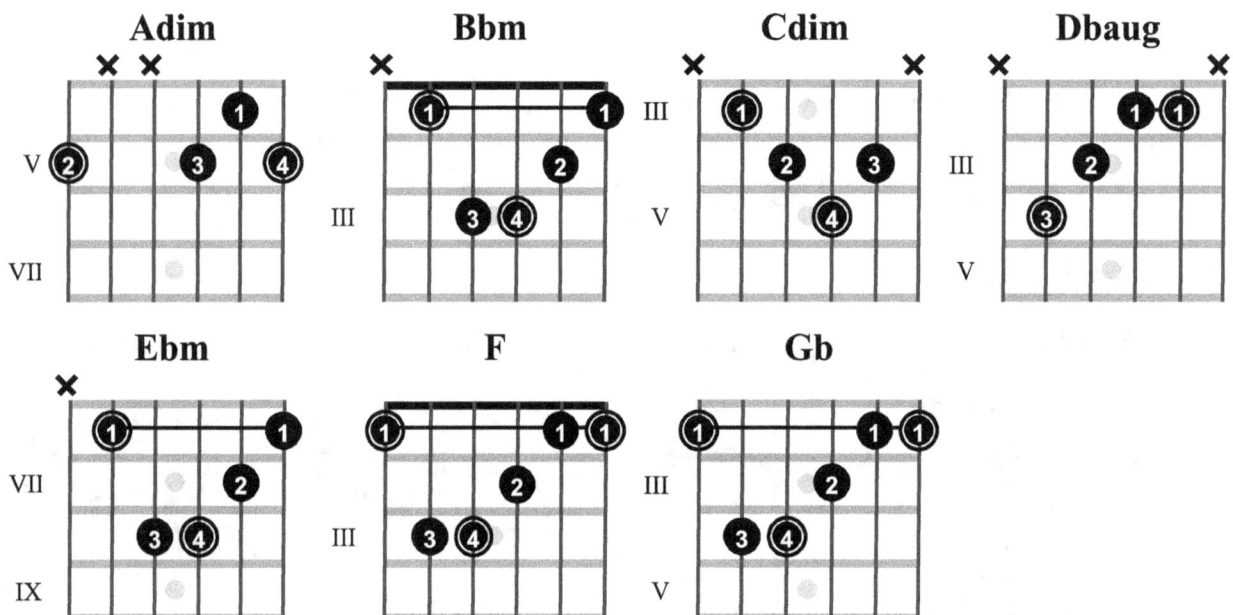

Adim   Bbm   Cdim   Dbaug

Ebm   F   Gb

7th Chords:

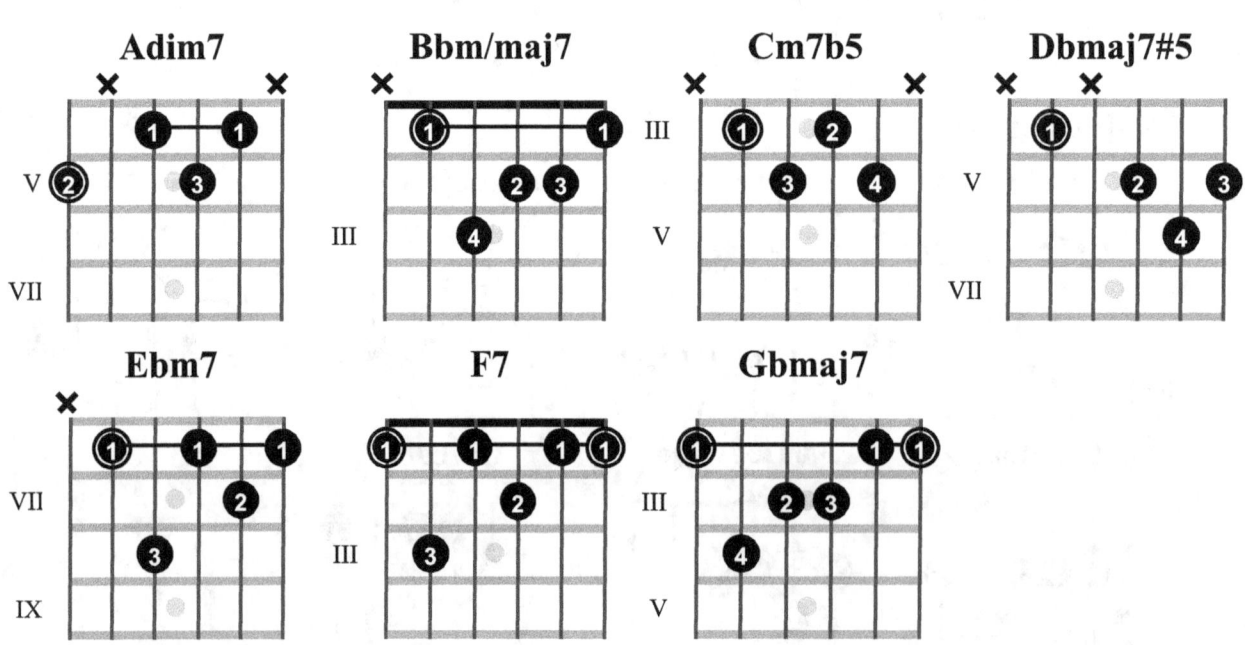

Adim7   Bbm/maj7   Cm7b5   Dbmaj7#5

Ebm7   F7   Gbmaj7

A Ultralocrian Scale
continued

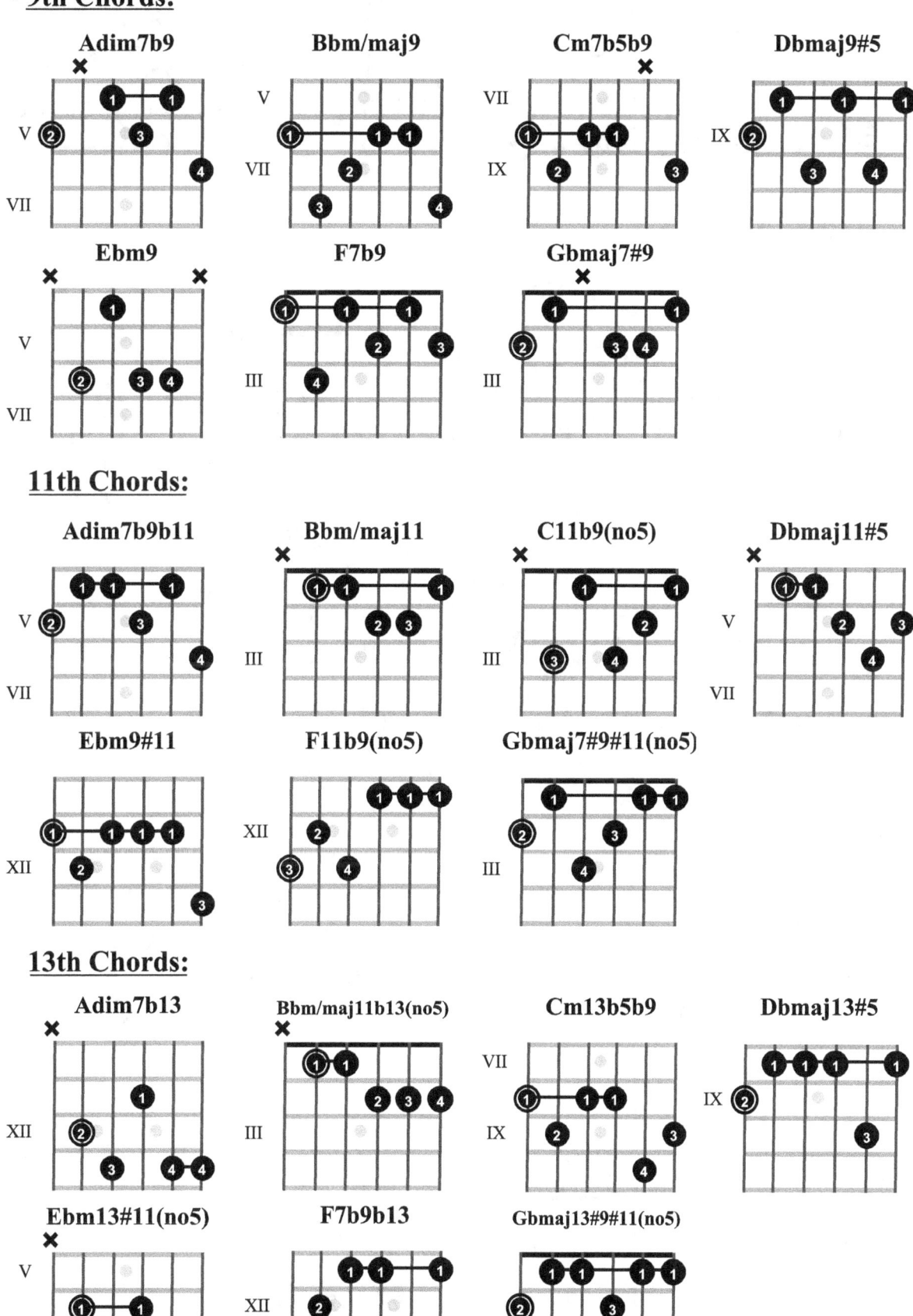

9th Chords:

Adim7b9 Bbm/maj9 Cm7b5b9 Dbmaj9#5

Ebm9 F7b9 Gbmaj7#9

11th Chords:

Adim7b9b11 Bbm/maj11 C11b9(no5) Dbmaj11#5

Ebm9#11 F11b9(no5) Gbmaj7#9#11(no5)

13th Chords:

Adim7b13 Bbm/maj11b13(no5) Cm13b5b9 Dbmaj13#5

Ebm13#11(no5) F7b9b13 Gbmaj13#9#11(no5)

A Melodic Minor Scale

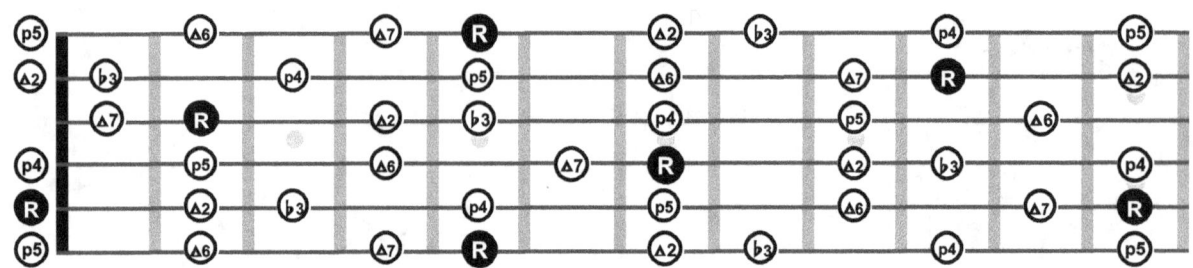

Triad Chords:

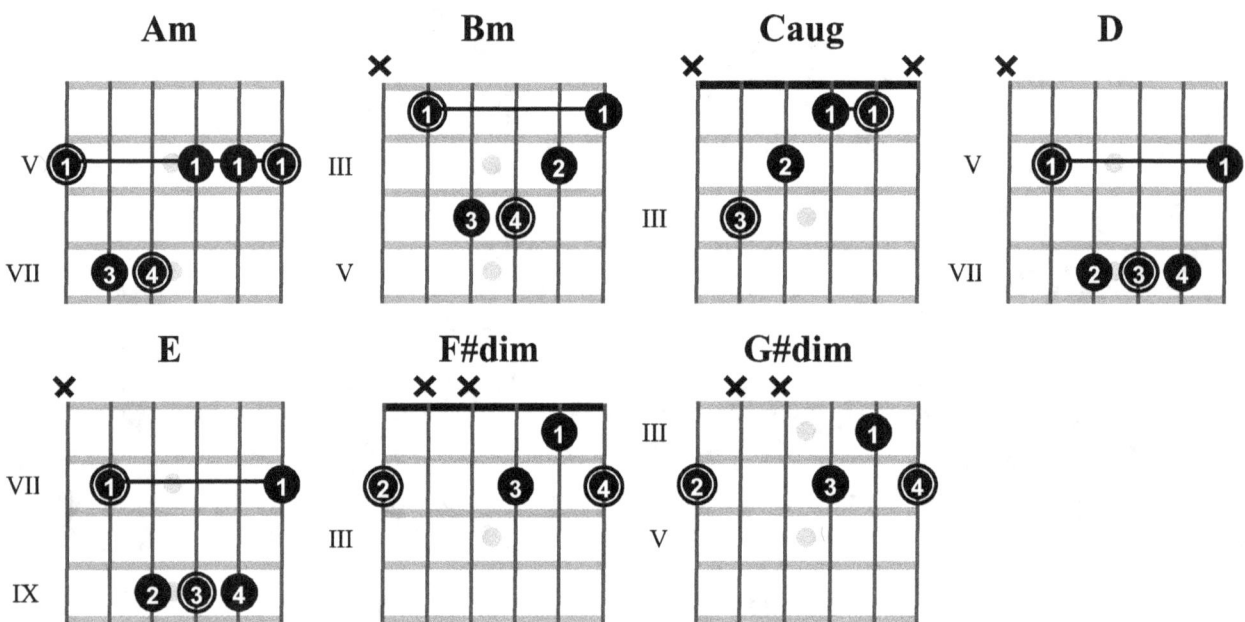

7th Chords:

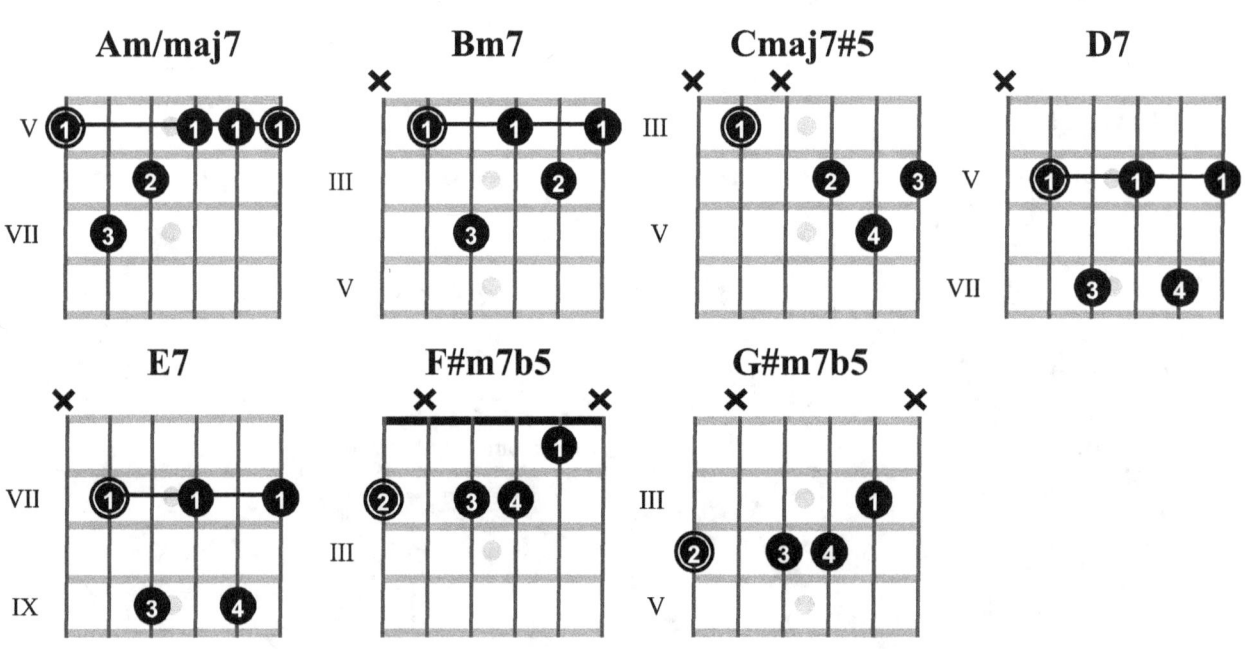

A Melodic Minor Scale
continued

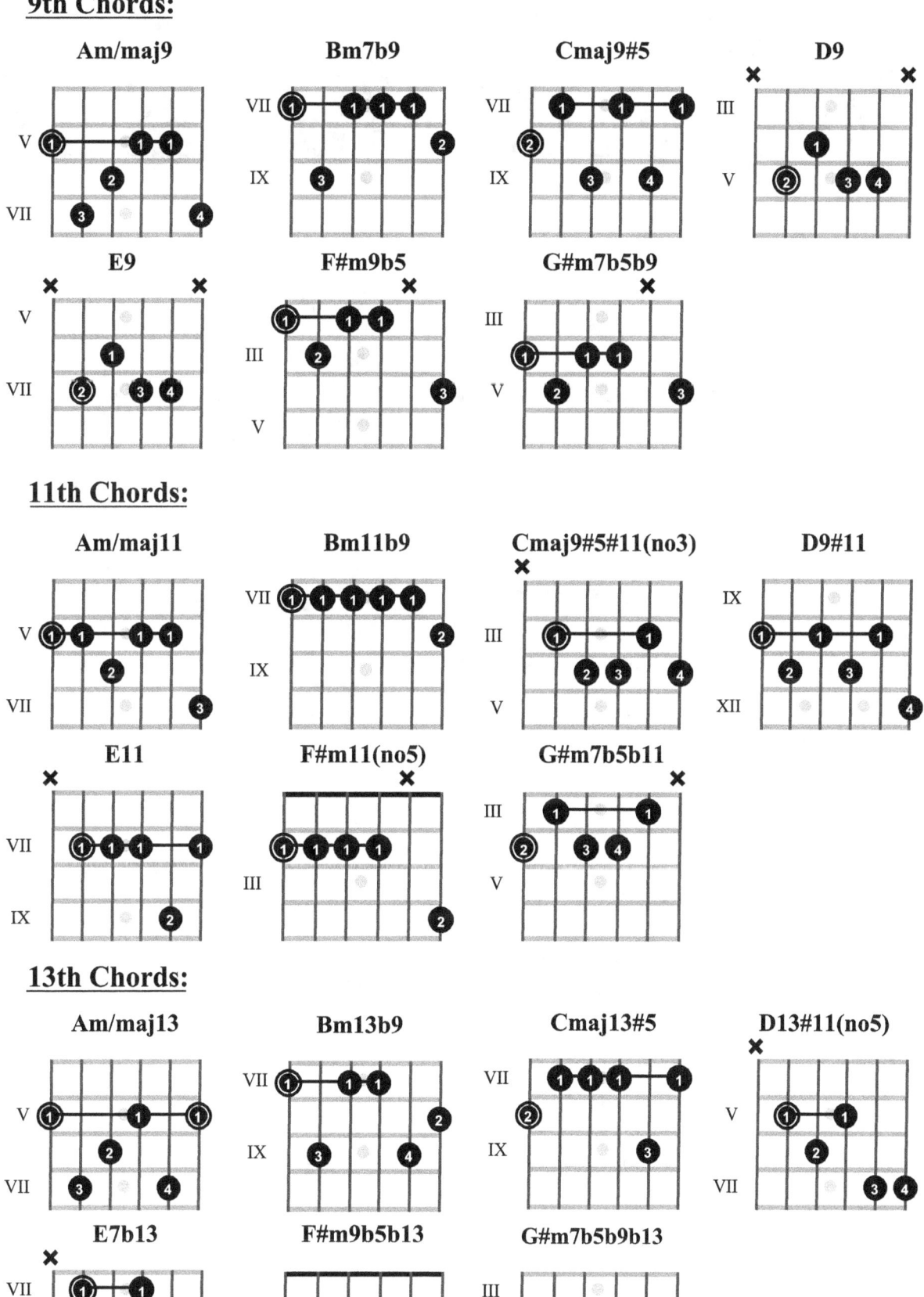

9th Chords:

Am/maj9 Bm7b9 Cmaj9#5 D9

E9 F#m9b5 G#m7b5b9

11th Chords:

Am/maj11 Bm11b9 Cmaj9#5#11(no3) D9#11

E11 F#m11(no5) G#m7b5b11

13th Chords:

Am/maj13 Bm13b9 Cmaj13#5 D13#11(no5)

E7b13 F#m9b5b13 G#m7b5b9b13

A Dorian b2 Scale

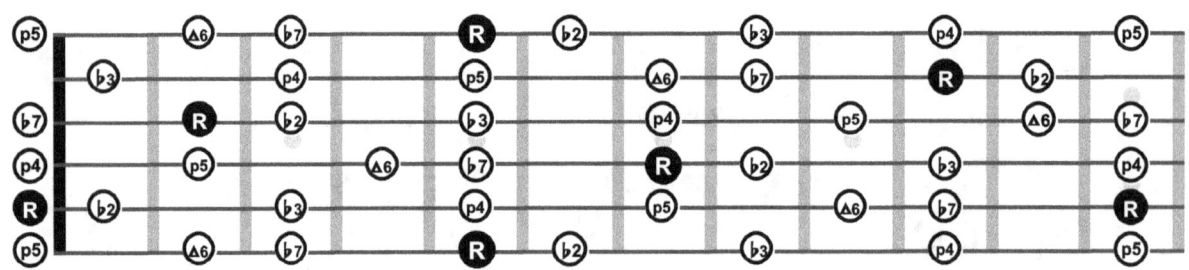

Triad Chords:

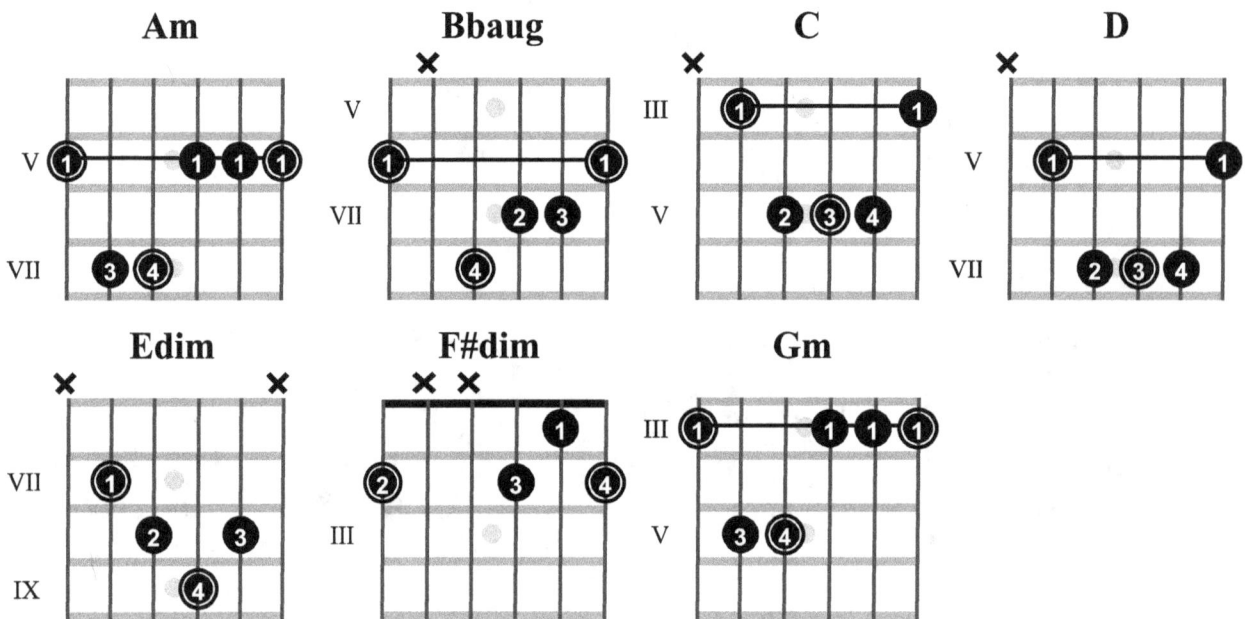

Am   Bbaug   C   D

Edim   F#dim   Gm

7th Chords:

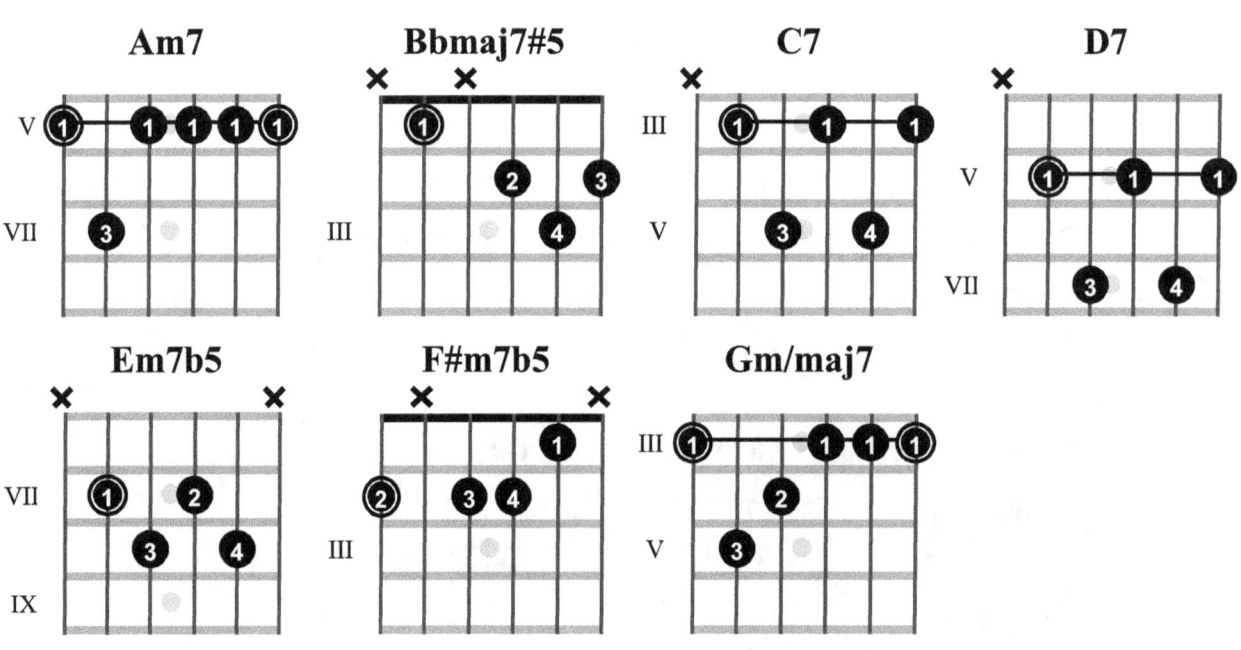

Am7   Bbmaj7#5   C7   D7

Em7b5   F#m7b5   Gm/maj7

A Dorian b2 Scale
continued

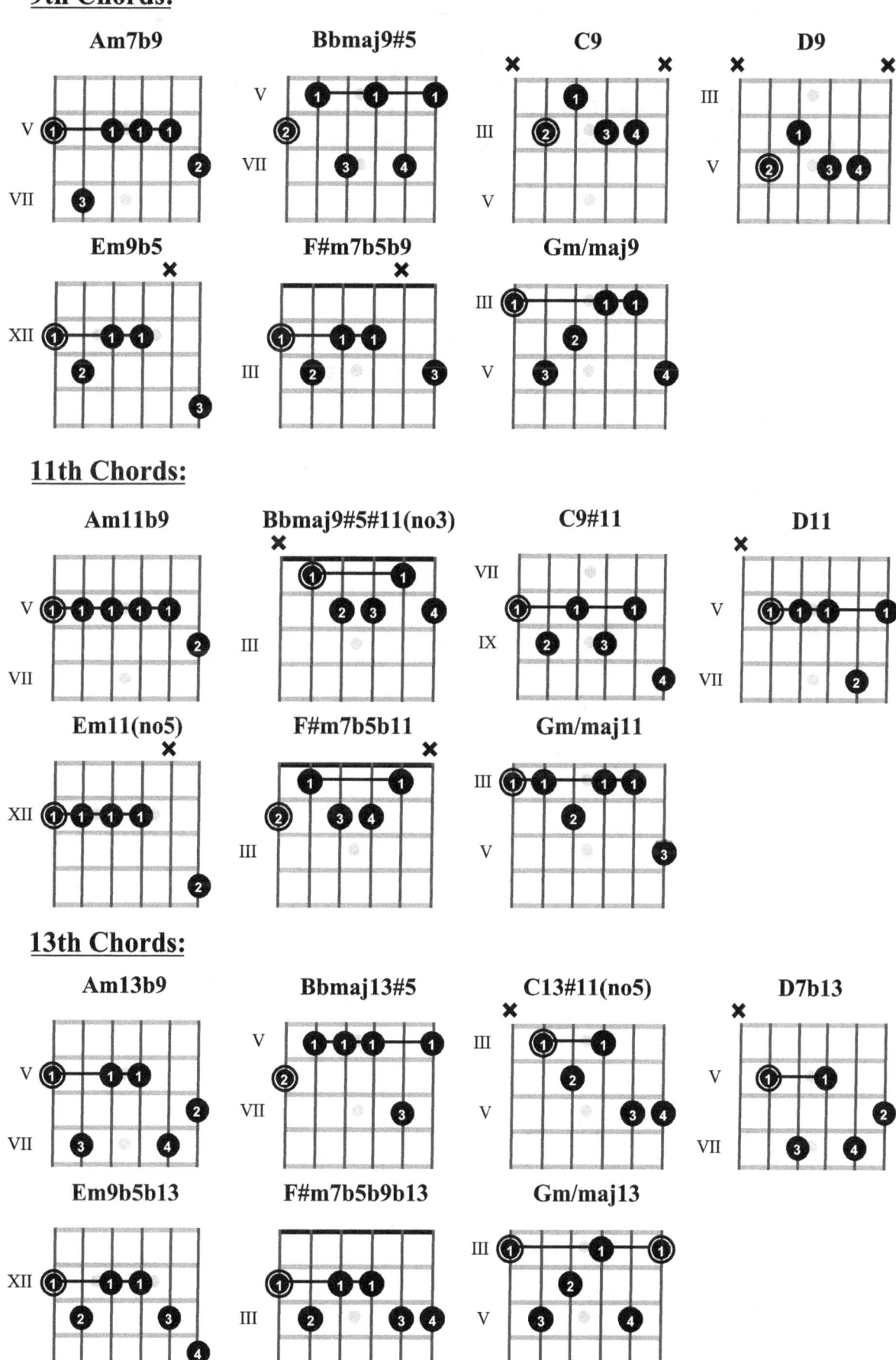

9th Chords:

Am7b9 Bbmaj9#5 C9 D9

Em9b5 F#m7b5b9 Gm/maj9

11th Chords:

Am11b9 Bbmaj9#5#11(no3) C9#11 D11

Em11(no5) F#m7b5b11 Gm/maj11

13th Chords:

Am13b9 Bbmaj13#5 C13#11(no5) D7b13

Em9b5b13 F#m7b5b9b13 Gm/maj13

A Lydian Augmented Scale

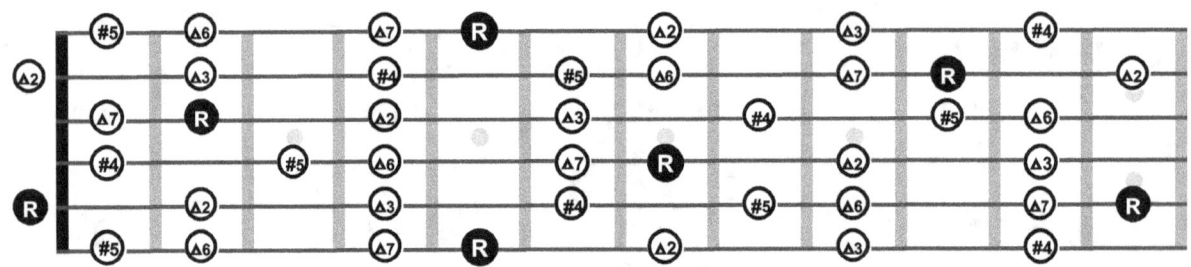

Triad Chords:

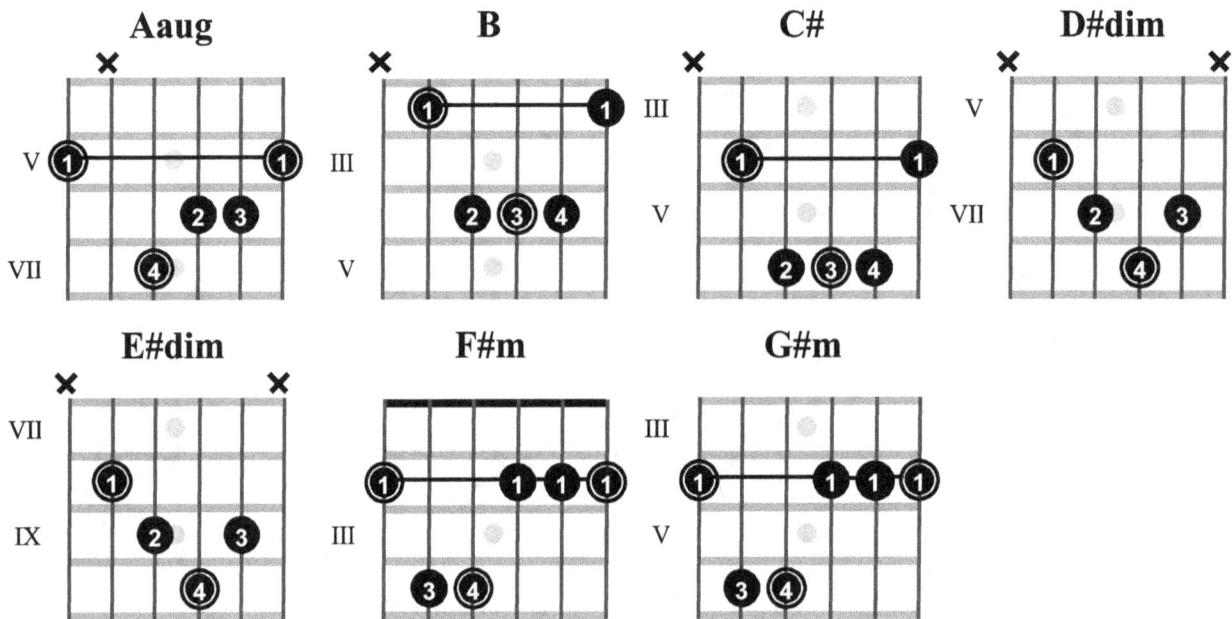

Aaug   B   C#   D#dim

E#dim   F#m   G#m

7th Chords:

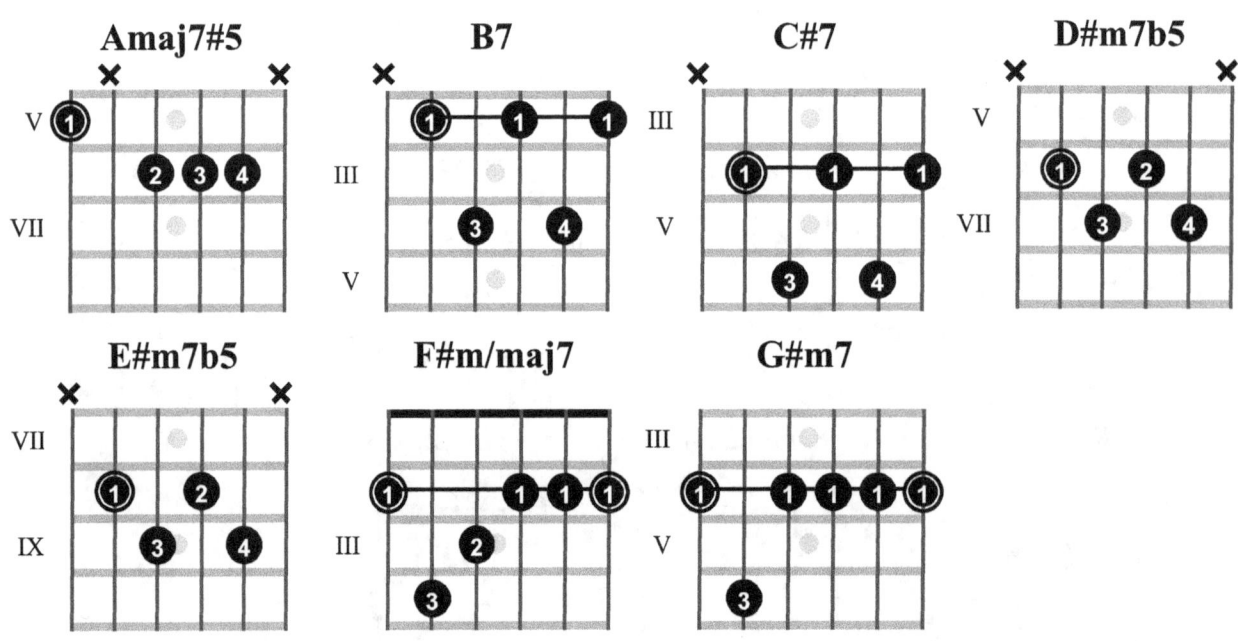

Amaj7#5   B7   C#7   D#m7b5

E#m7b5   F#m/maj7   G#m7

A Lydian Augmented Scale
continued

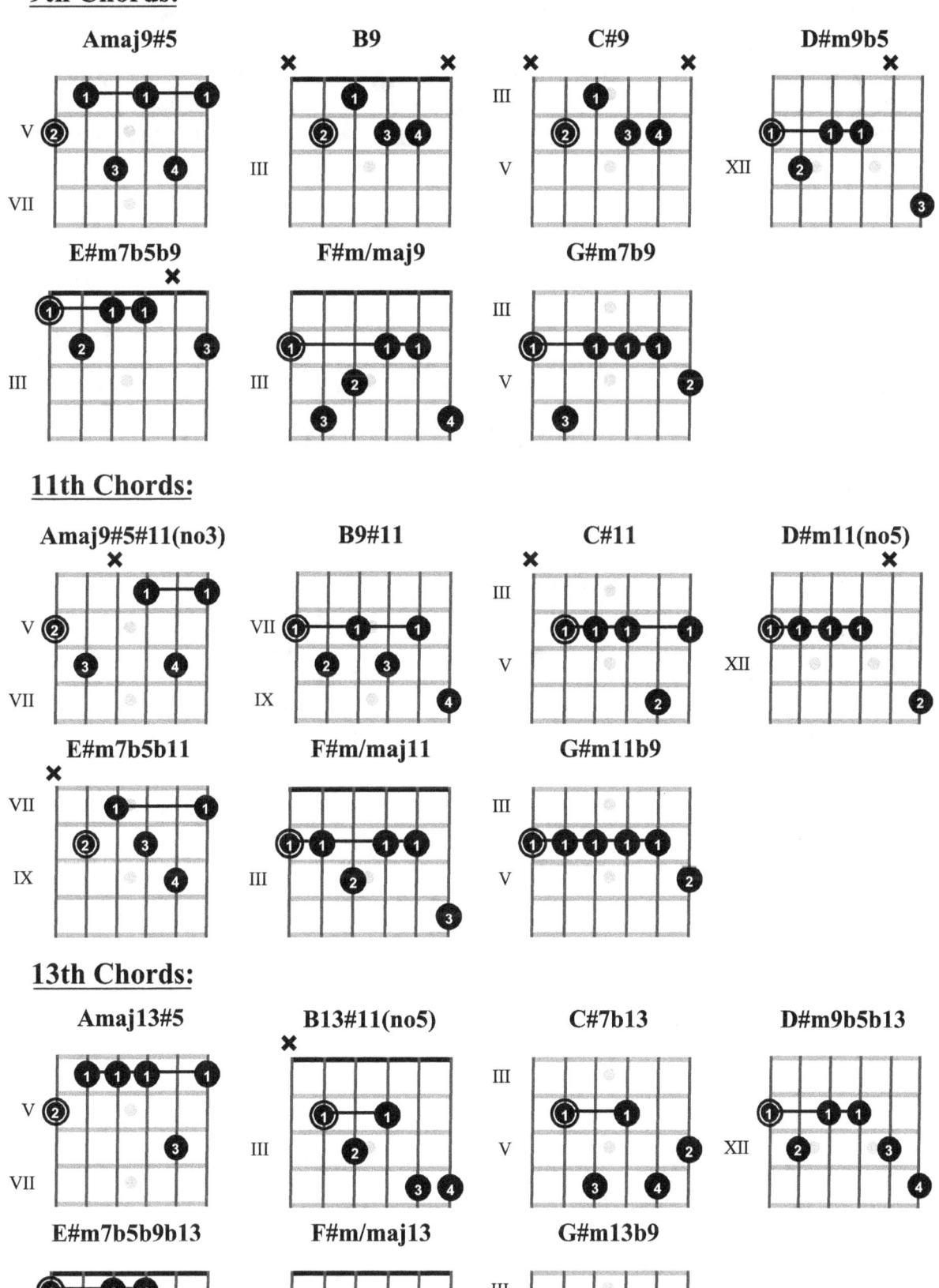

9th Chords:

Amaj9#5 B9 C#9 D#m9b5

E#m7b5b9 F#m/maj9 G#m7b9

11th Chords:

Amaj9#5#11(no3) B9#11 C#11 D#m11(no5)

E#m7b5b11 F#m/maj11 G#m11b9

13th Chords:

Amaj13#5 B13#11(no5) C#7b13 D#m9b5b13

E#m7b5b9b13 F#m/maj13 G#m13b9

A Lydian Dominant Scale

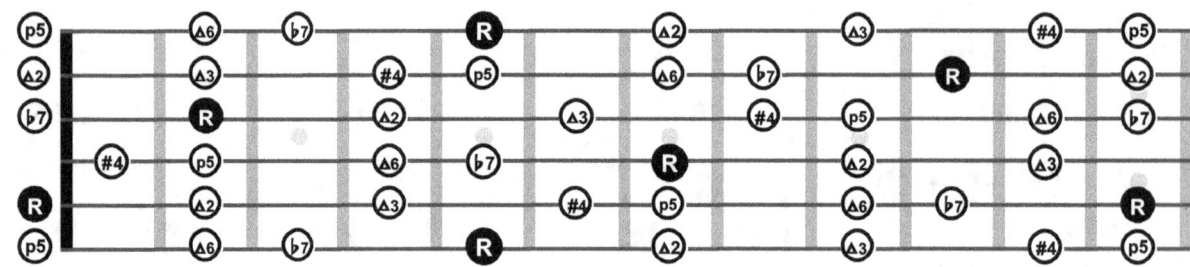

Triad Chords:

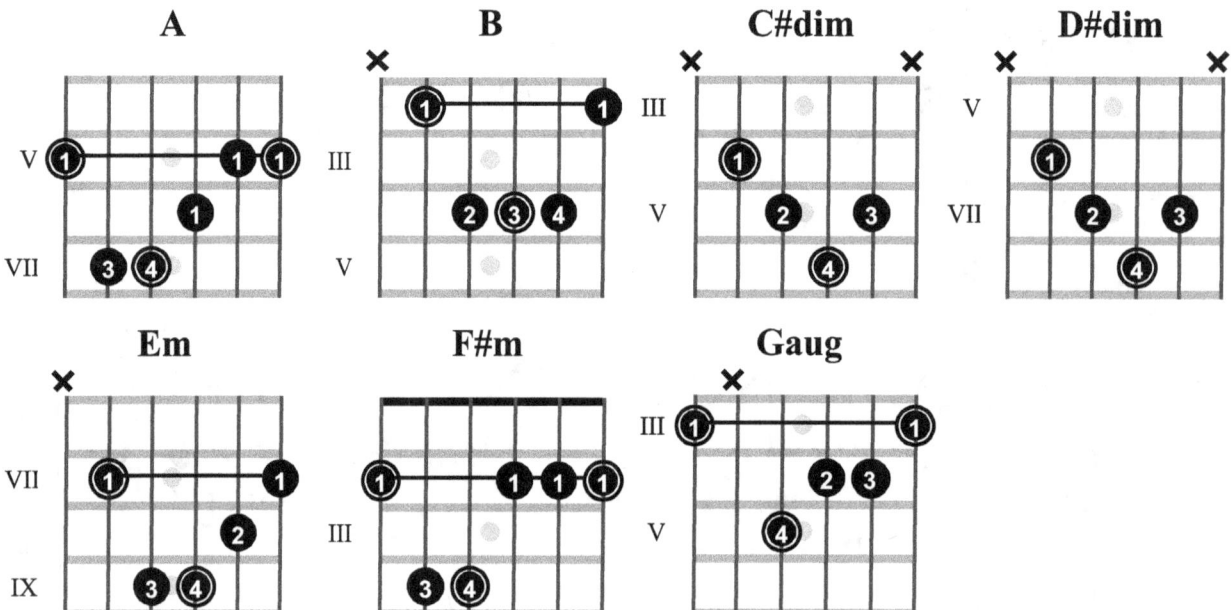

7th Chords:

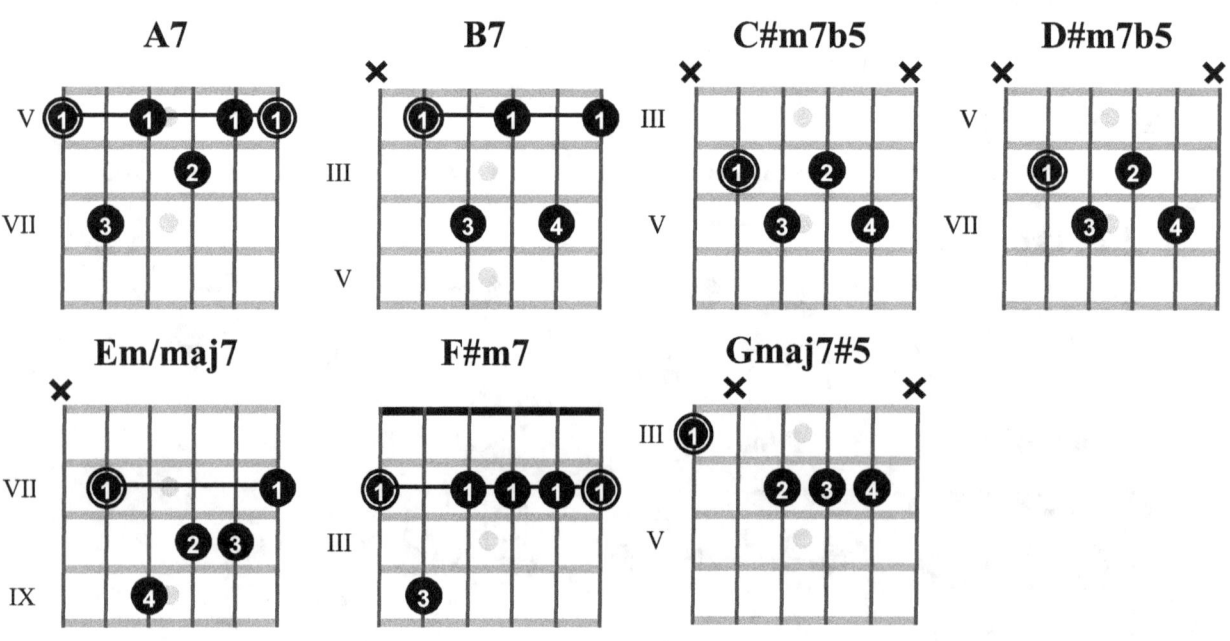

A Lydian Dominant Scale
continued

9th Chords:

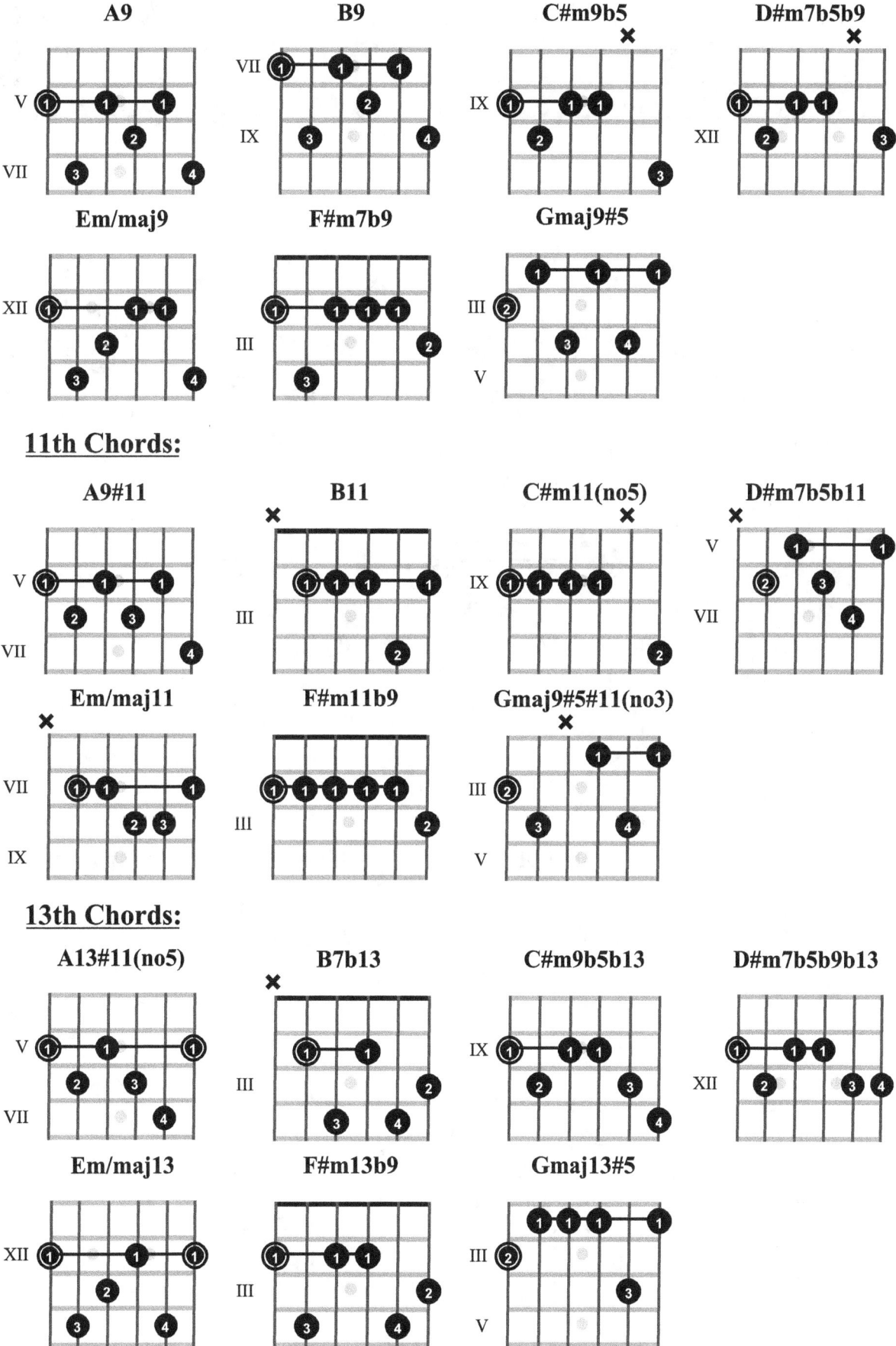

A9

B9

C#m9b5

D#m7b5b9

Em/maj9

F#m7b9

Gmaj9#5

11th Chords:

A9#11

B11

C#m11(no5)

D#m7b5b11

Em/maj11

F#m11b9

Gmaj9#5#11(no3)

13th Chords:

A13#11(no5)

B7b13

C#m9b5b13

D#m7b5b9b13

Em/maj13

F#m13b9

Gmaj13#5

A Mixolydian b6 Scale

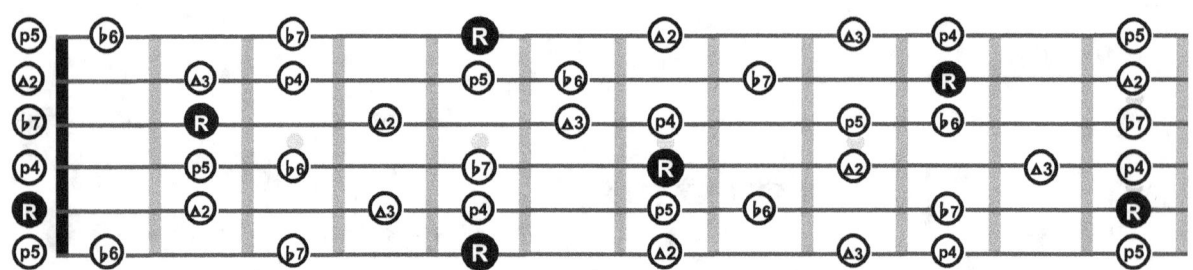

Triad Chords:

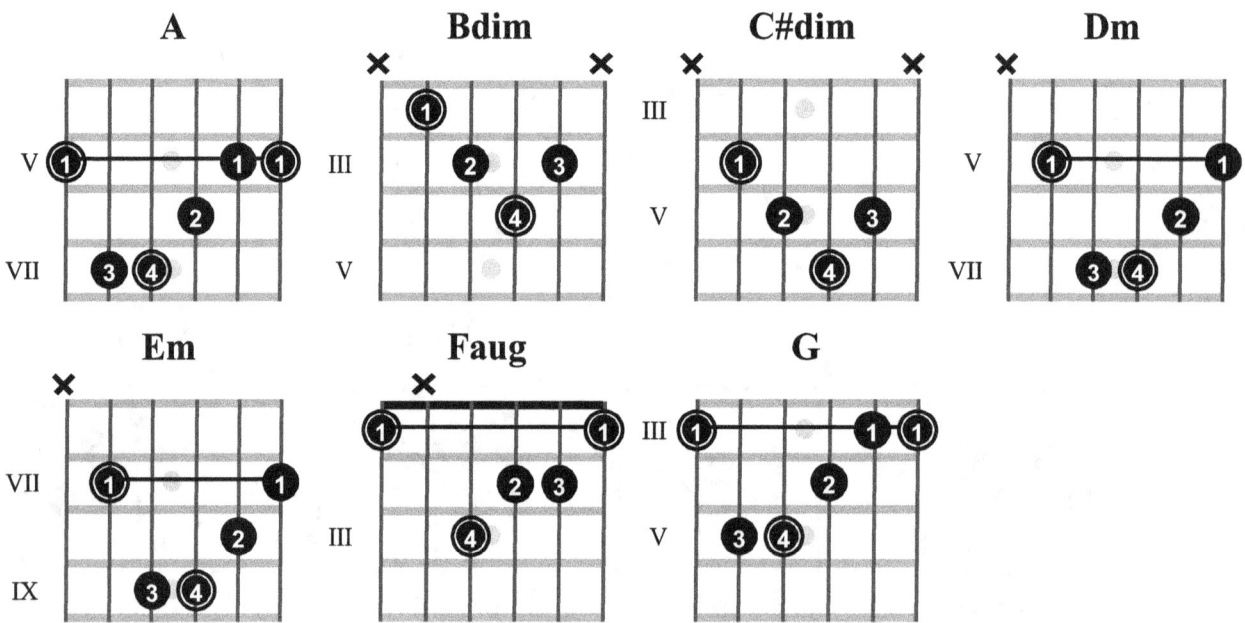

7th Chords:

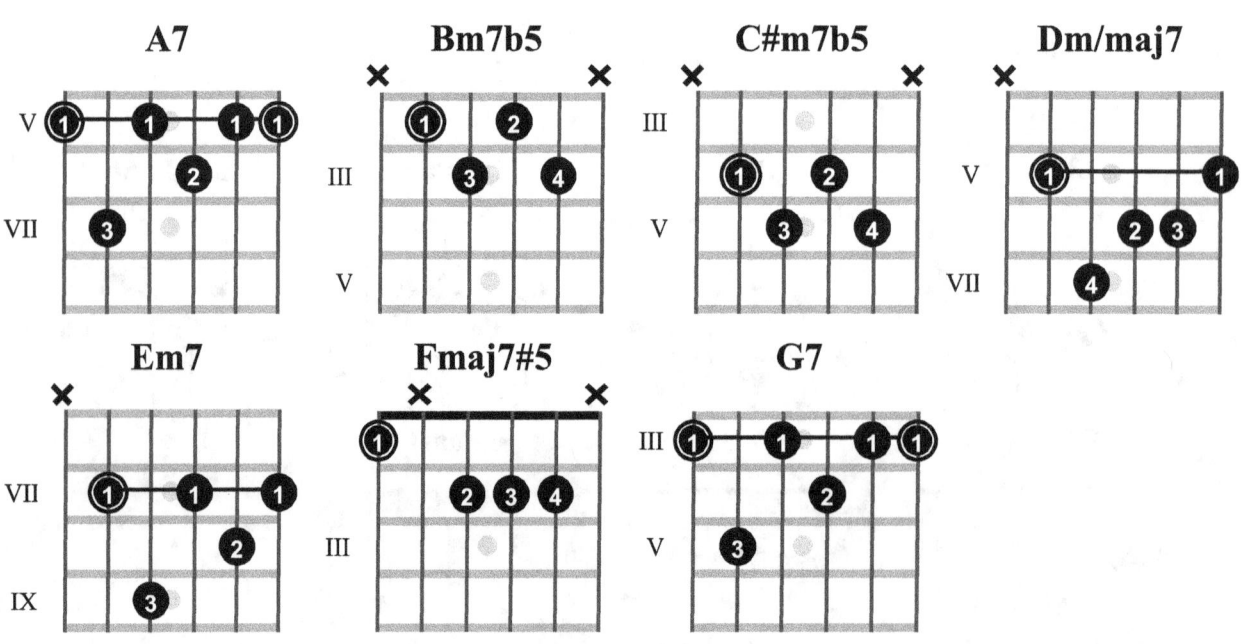

A Mixolydian b6 Scale
continued

9th Chords:

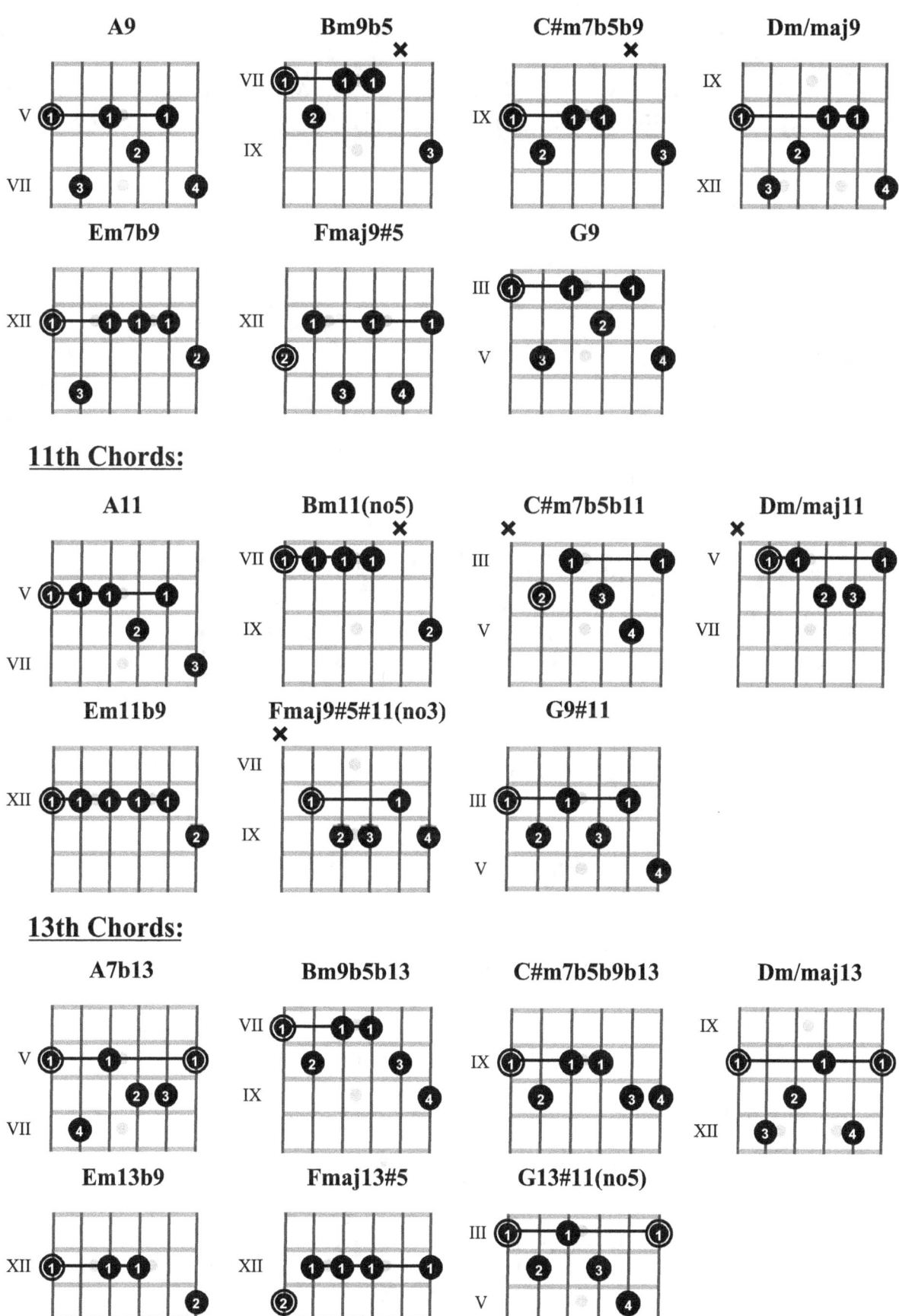

A9   Bm9b5   C#m7b5b9   Dm/maj9

Em7b9   Fmaj9#5   G9

11th Chords:

A11   Bm11(no5)   C#m7b5b11   Dm/maj11

Em11b9   Fmaj9#5#11(no3)   G9#11

13th Chords:

A7b13   Bm9b5b13   C#m7b5b9b13   Dm/maj13

Em13b9   Fmaj13#5   G13#11(no5)

A Locrian #2 Scale

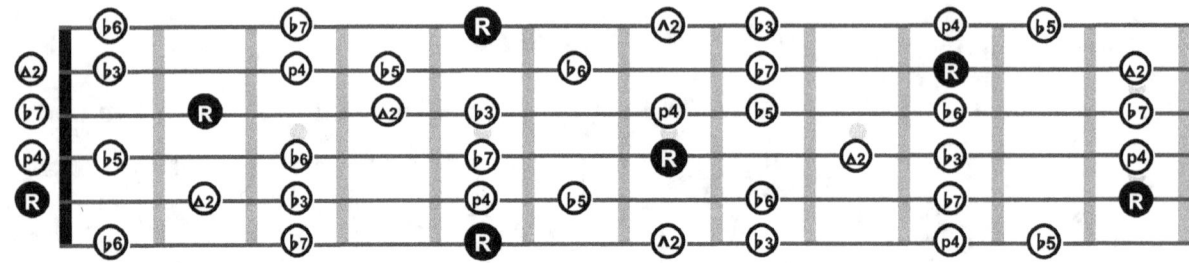

Triad Chords:

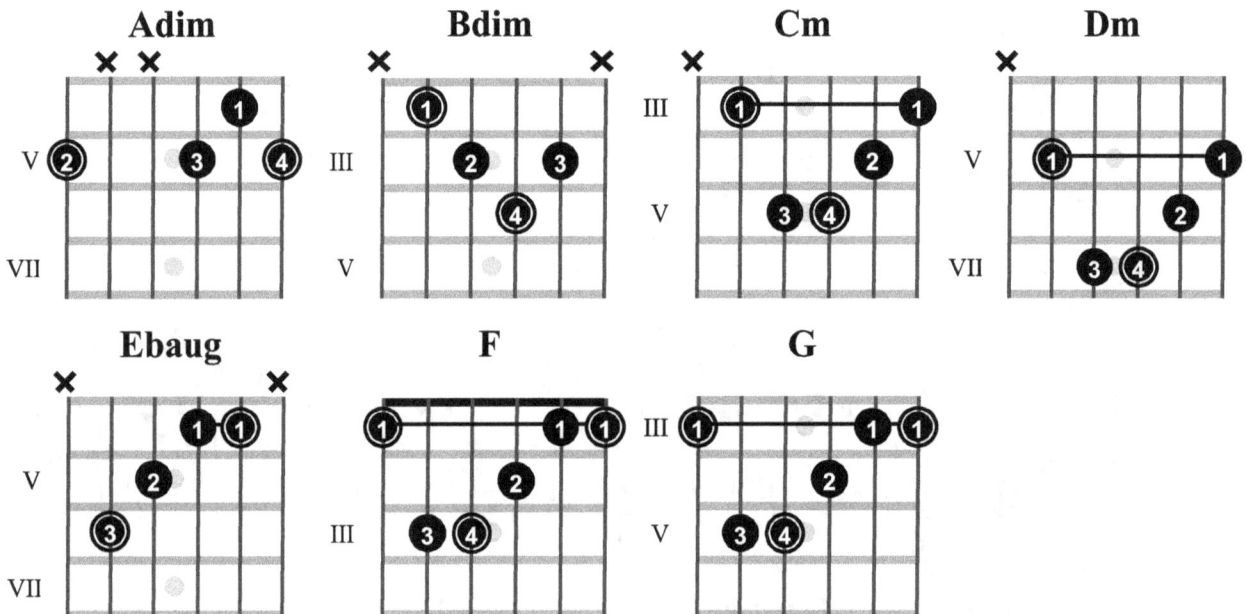

Adim   Bdim   Cm   Dm

Ebaug   F   G

7th Chords:

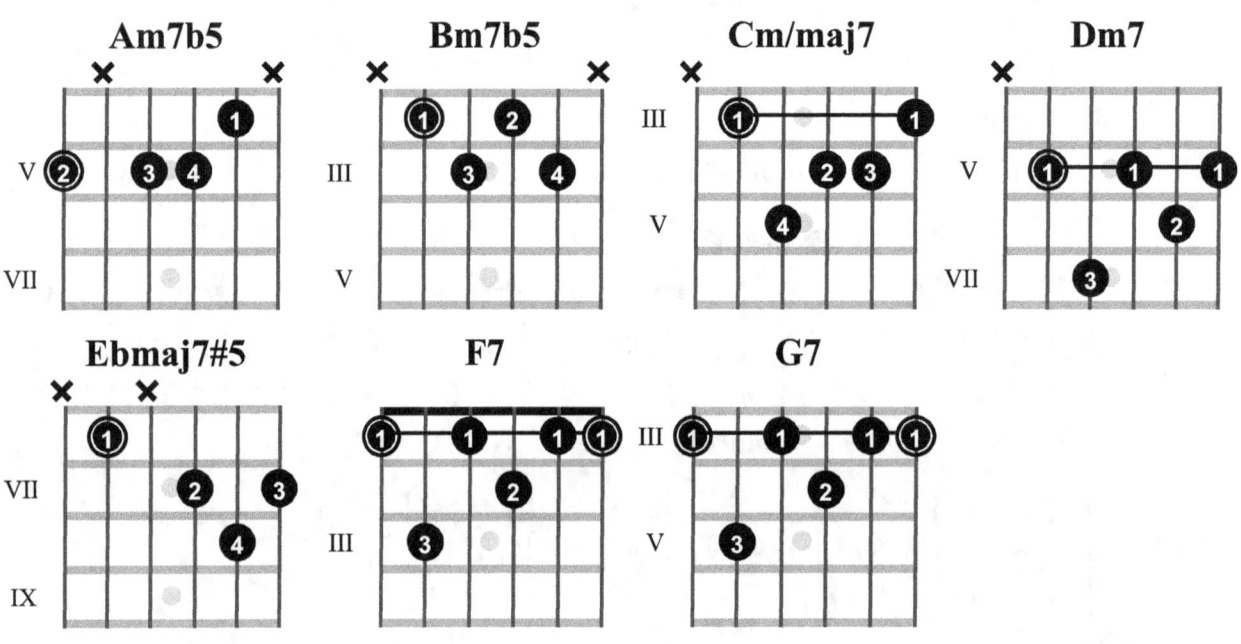

Am7b5   Bm7b5   Cm/maj7   Dm7

Ebmaj7#5   F7   G7

A Locrian #2 Scale
continued

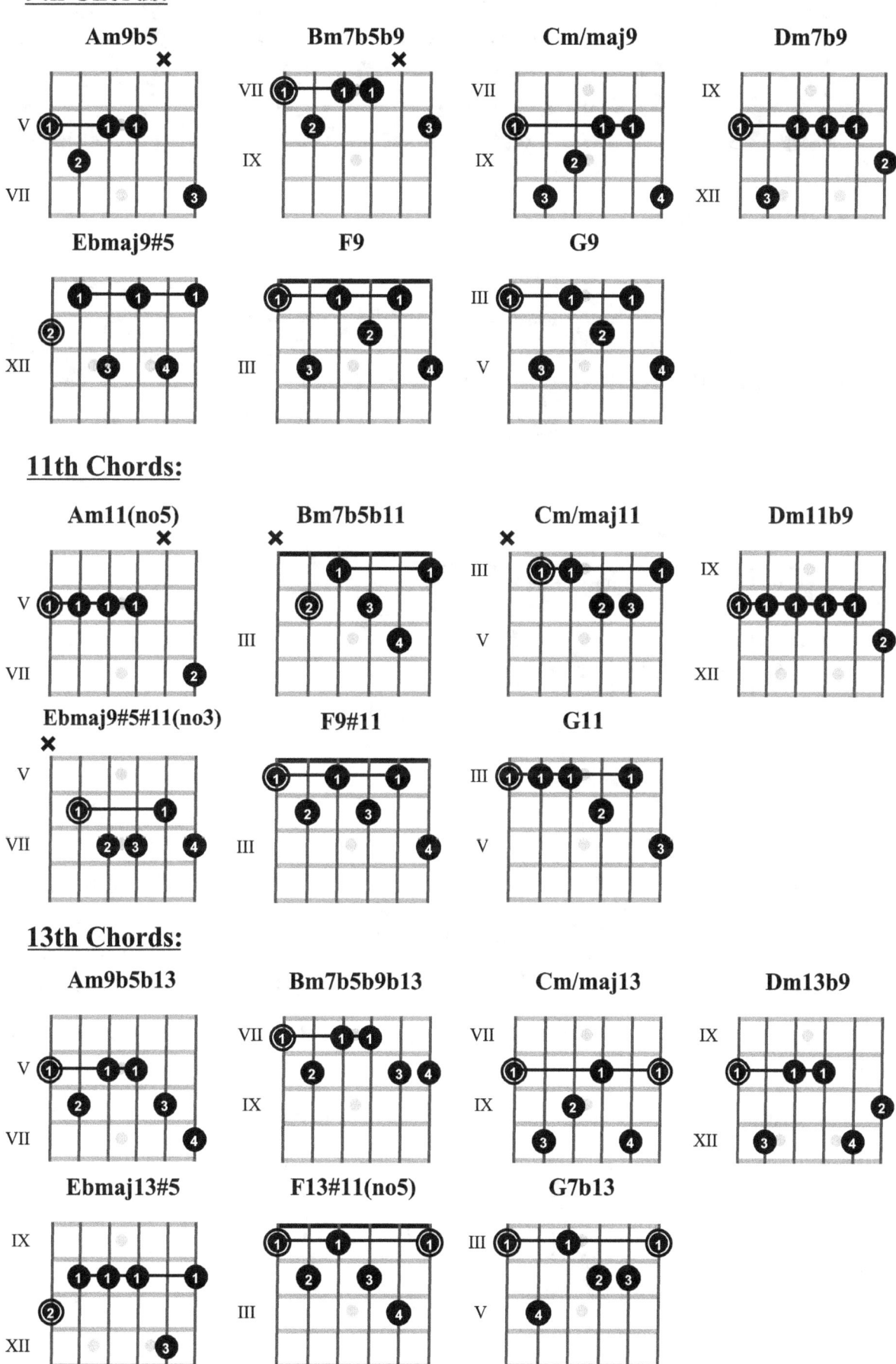

9th Chords:

Am9b5   Bm7b5b9   Cm/maj9   Dm7b9

Ebmaj9#5   F9   G9

11th Chords:

Am11(no5)   Bm7b5b11   Cm/maj11   Dm11b9

Ebmaj9#5#11(no3)   F9#11   G11

13th Chords:

Am9b5b13   Bm7b5b9b13   Cm/maj13   Dm13b9

Ebmaj13#5   F13#11(no5)   G7b13

A Altered Scale

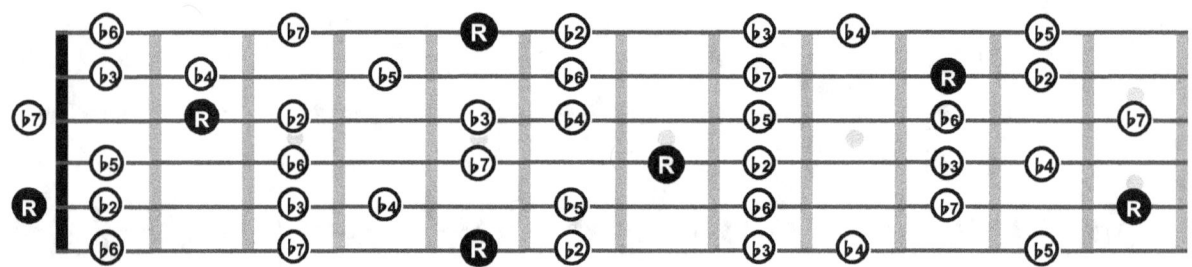

Triad Chords:

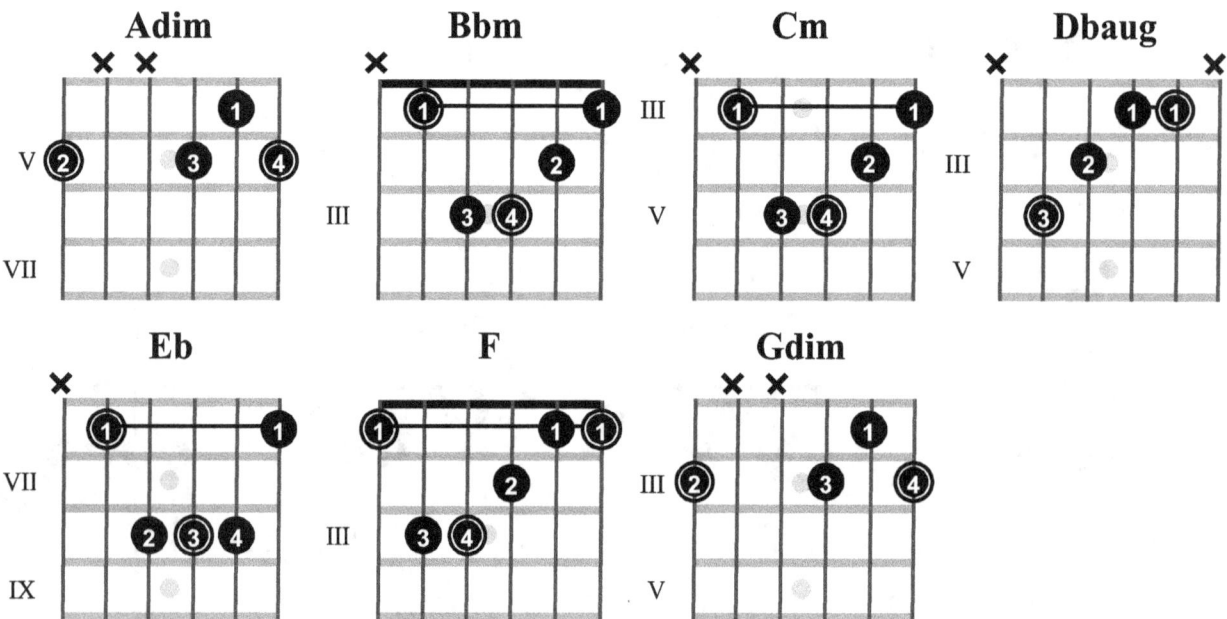

Adim   Bbm   Cm   Dbaug

Eb   F   Gdim

7th Chords:

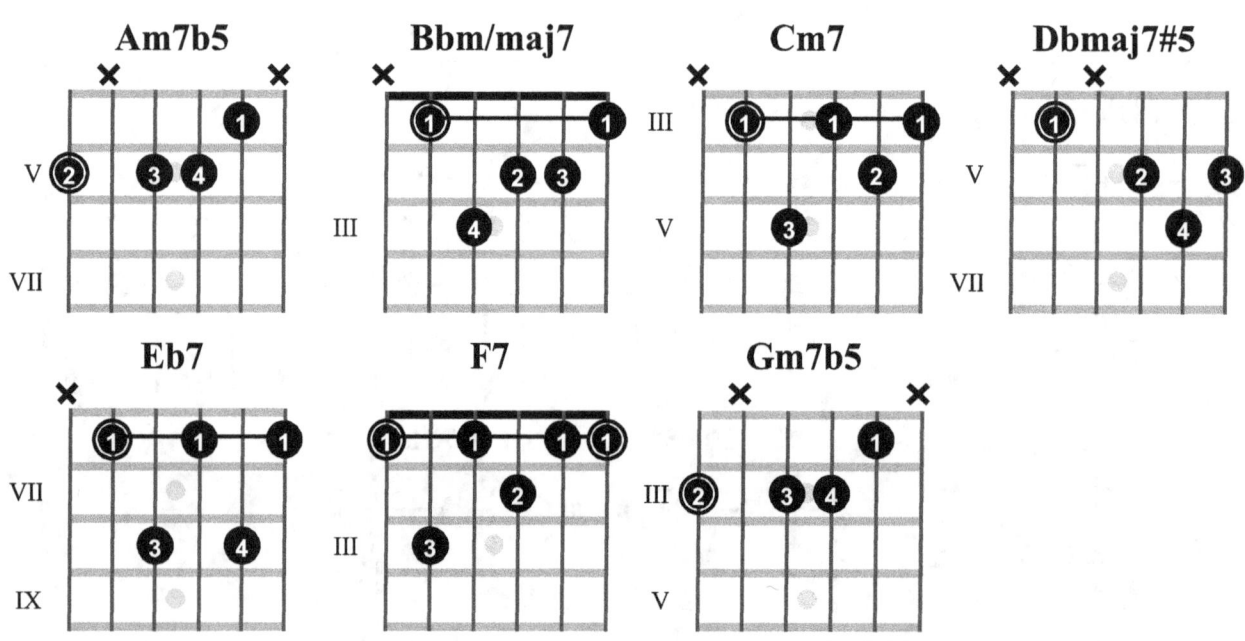

Am7b5   Bbm/maj7   Cm7   Dbmaj7#5

Eb7   F7   Gm7b5

A Altered Scale
continued

9th Chords:

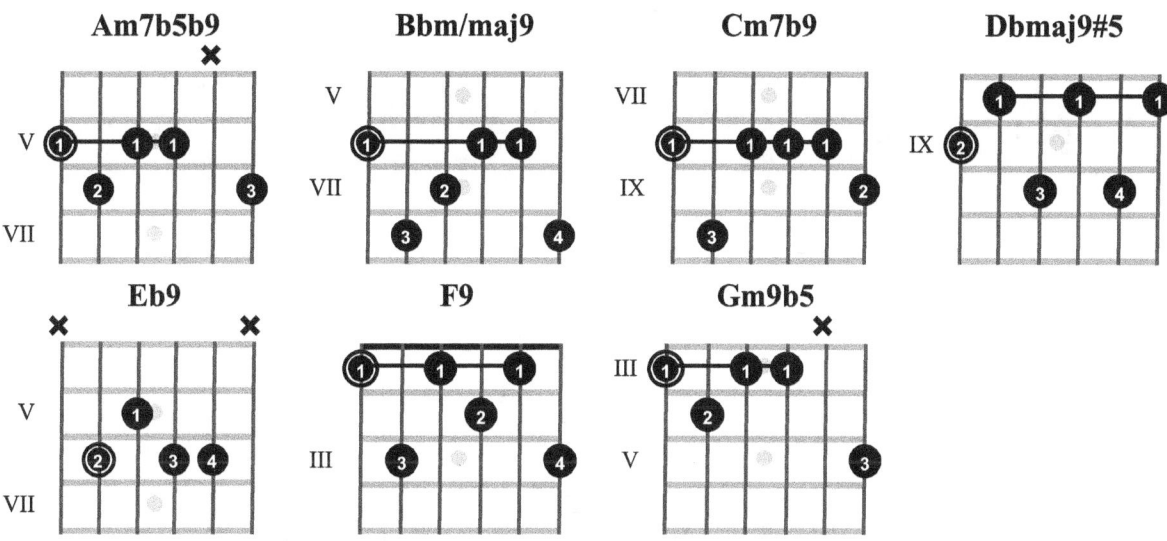

11th Chords:

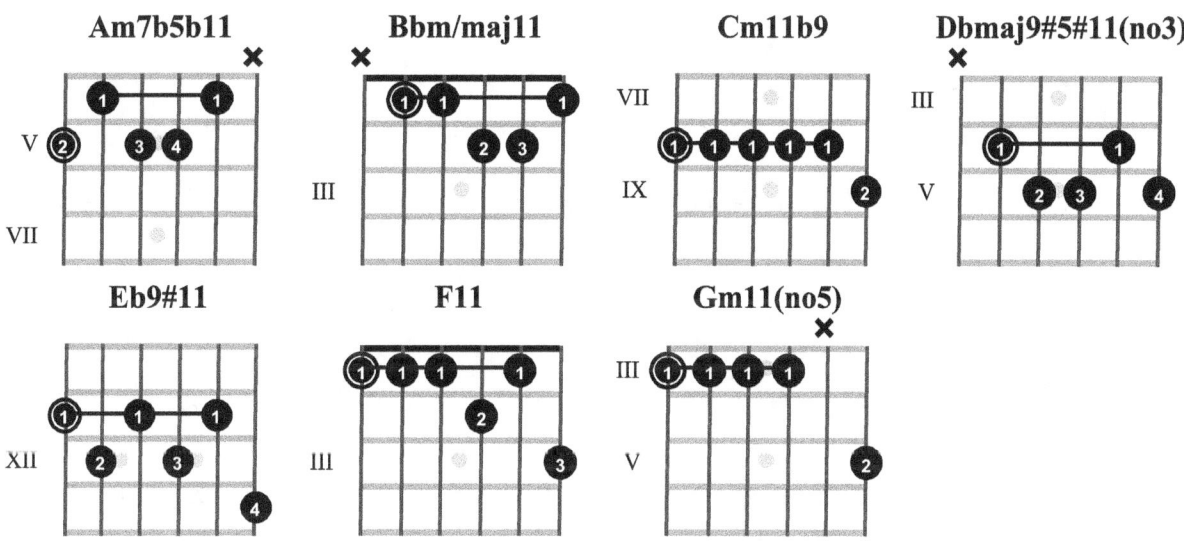

13th Chords:

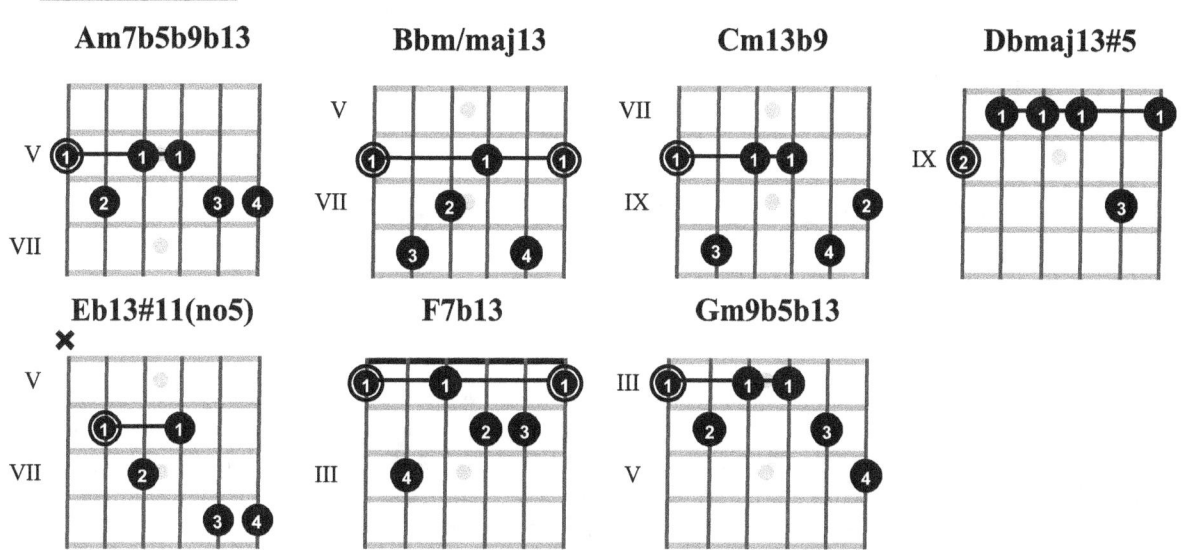

Harmonization Index

A Major Scale

Triad Chords:

A - Bm - C#m - D - E - F#m - G#dim

7th Chords:

Amaj7 - Bm7 - C#m7 - Dmaj7 - E7 - F#m7 - G#dim7b5

9th Chords:

Amaj9 - Bm9 - C#m7b9 - Dmaj9 - E9 - F#m9 - G#m7b5b9

11th Chords:

Amaj11 - Bm11 - C#m11b9 - Dmaj9#11 - E11 - F#m11 - G#m11b5b9

13th Chords:

Amaj13 - Bm13 - C#m11b9b13 - Dmaj13#11 - E13 - F#m11b13 - G#m11b5b9b13

"In practice the extended chord grips on the guitar cannot include all of the necessary intervals. For example, on the 13th chord, the 11th and maybe the 9th or the 5th are excluded. So, we present this index to demonstrate all the intervals included in every harmonized chord up to the 13th extension providing a detailed insight to the complete theoretical foundation."

Harmonization Index

A Harmonic Minor Scale

Triad Chords:

Am - Bdim - Caug - Dm - E - F - G#dim

7th Chords:

Am/maj7 - Bm7b5 - Cmaj7#5 - Dm7 - E7 - Fmaj7 - G#dim7

9th Chords:

Am/maj9 - Bm7b5b9 - Cmaj9#5 - Dm9 - E7b9 - Fmaj7#9 - G#dim7b9

11th Chords:

Am/maj11 - Bm11b5b9 - Cmaj11#5 - Dm9#11 - E11b9 - Fmaj7#9#11 - G#dim7b9b11

13th Chords:

Am/maj11b13 - Bm13b5b9 - Cmaj13#5 - Dm13#11 - E11b9b13 - Fmaj13#9#11 - G#dim7b9b11b13

Harmonization Index

A Melodic Minor Scale

Triad Chords:

Am - Bm - Caug - D - E - F#dim - G#dim

7th Chords:

Am/maj7 - Bm7 - Cmaj7#5 - D7 - E7 - F#m7b5 - G#m7b5

9th Chords:

Am/maj9 - Bm7b9 - Cmaj9#5 - D9 - E9 - F#m9b5 - G#m7b5b9

11th Chords:

Am/maj11 - Bm11b9 - Cmaj9#5#11 - D9#11 - E11 - F#m11b5 - G#m7b5b9b11

13th Chords:

Am/maj13 - Bm13b9 - Cmaj13#5#11 - D13#11 - E11b13 - F#m11b5b13 - G#m7b5b9b11b13

A Ionian Scale

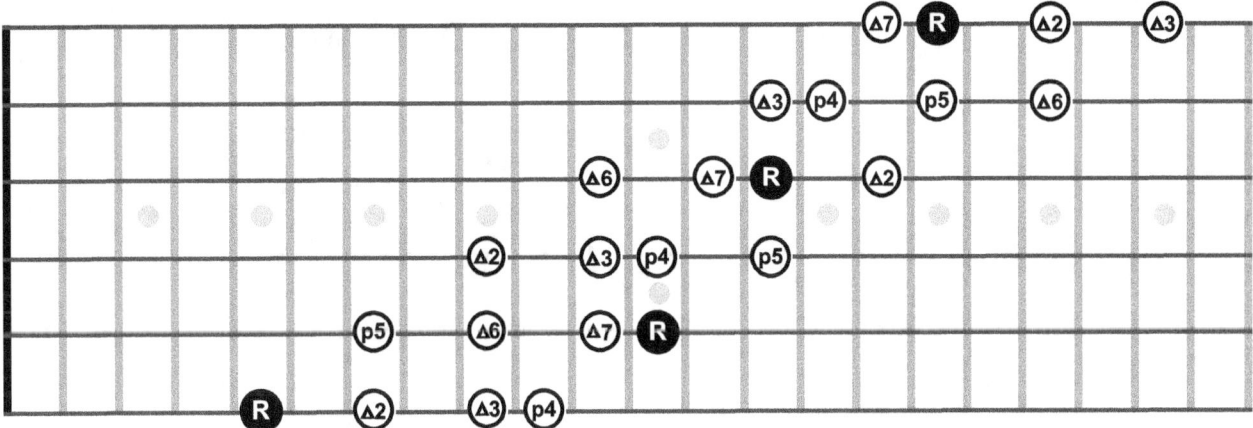

A Dorian Scale

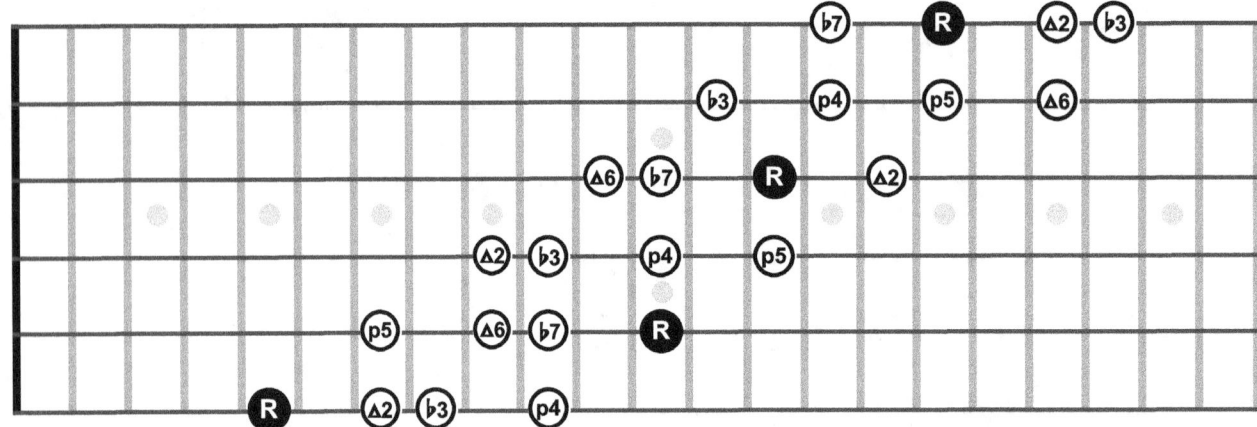

A Phrygian Scale

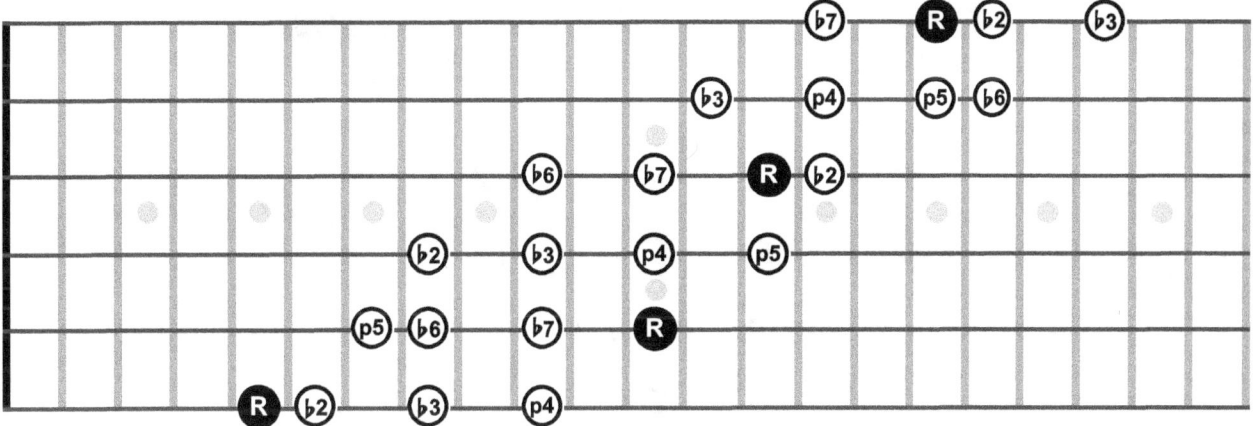

A Lydian Scale

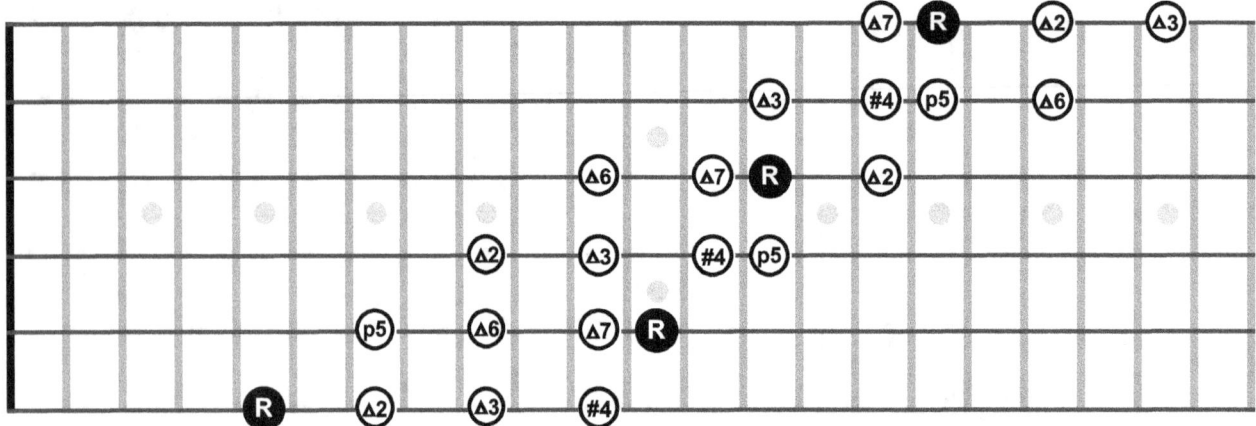

A Mixolydian Scale

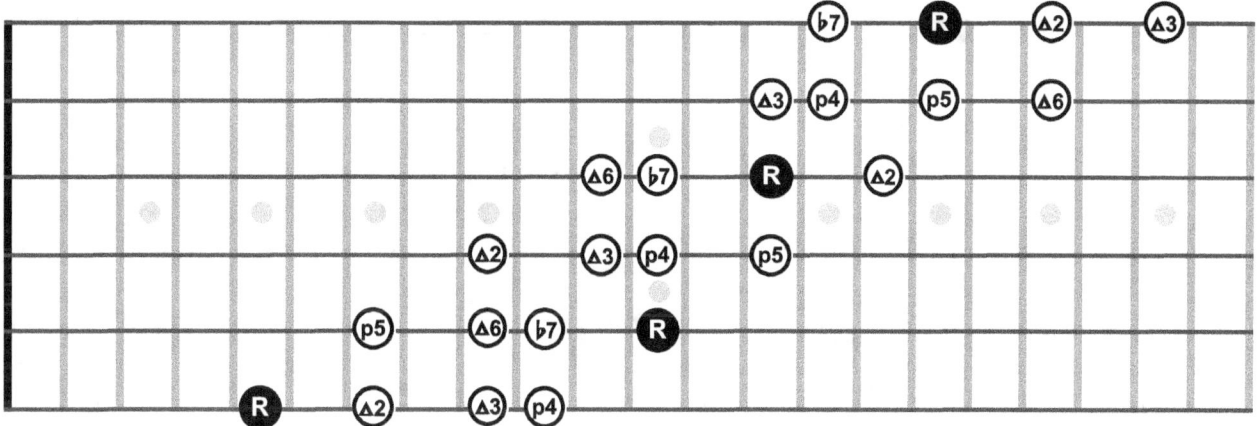

A Aeolian Scale

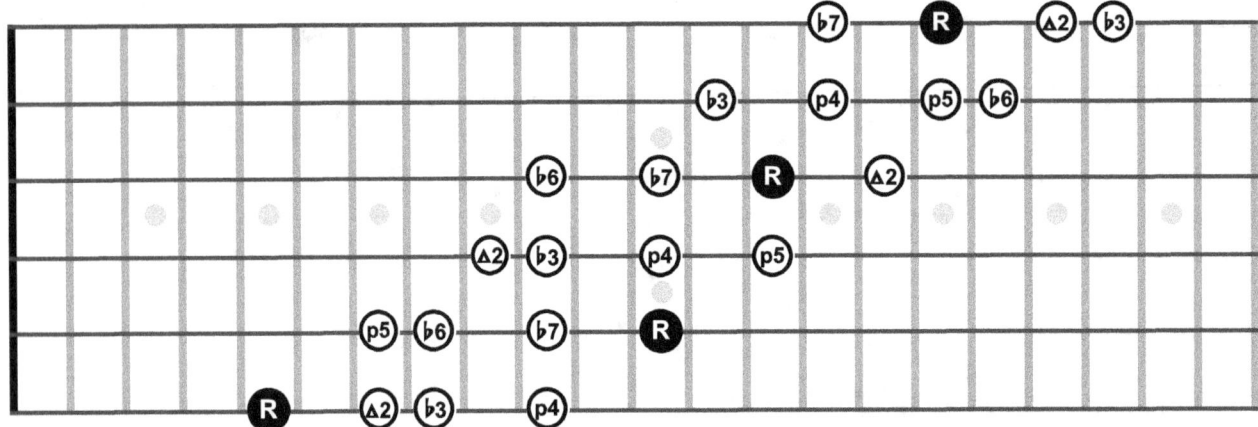

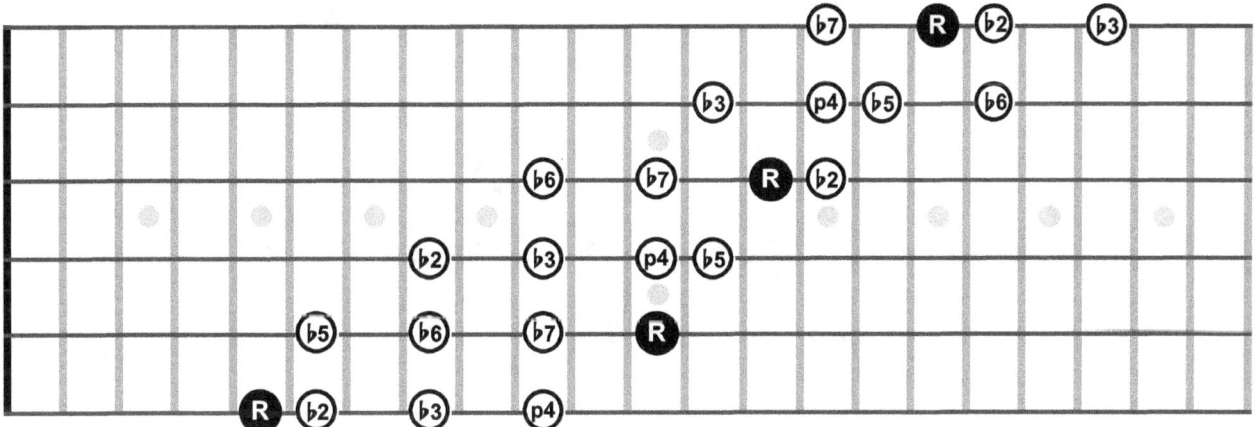

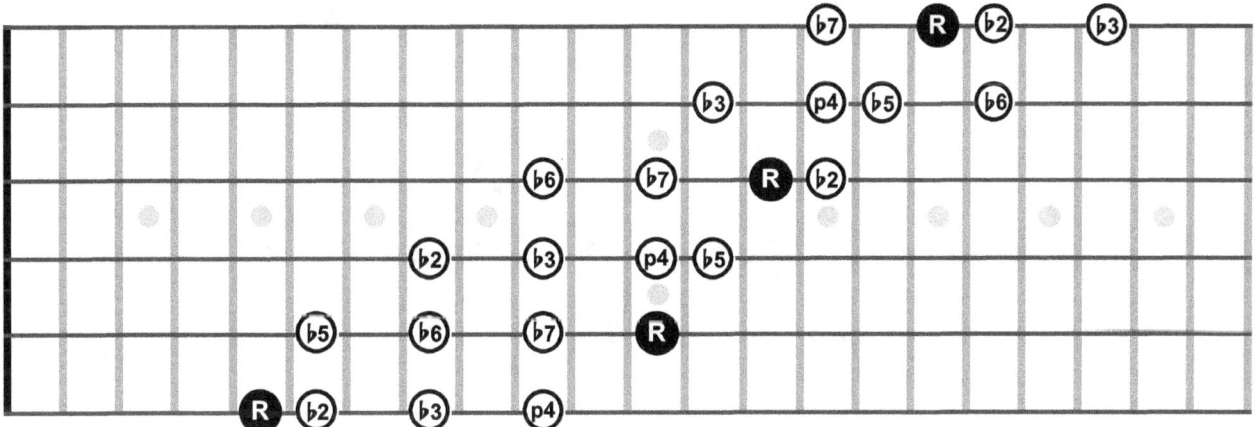

A Locrian Scale

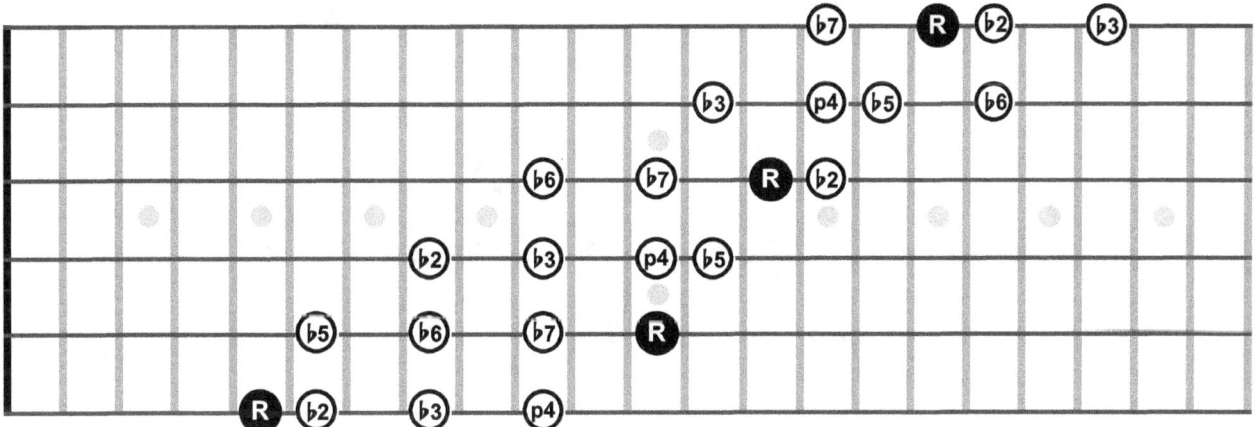

A Harmonic Minor Scale

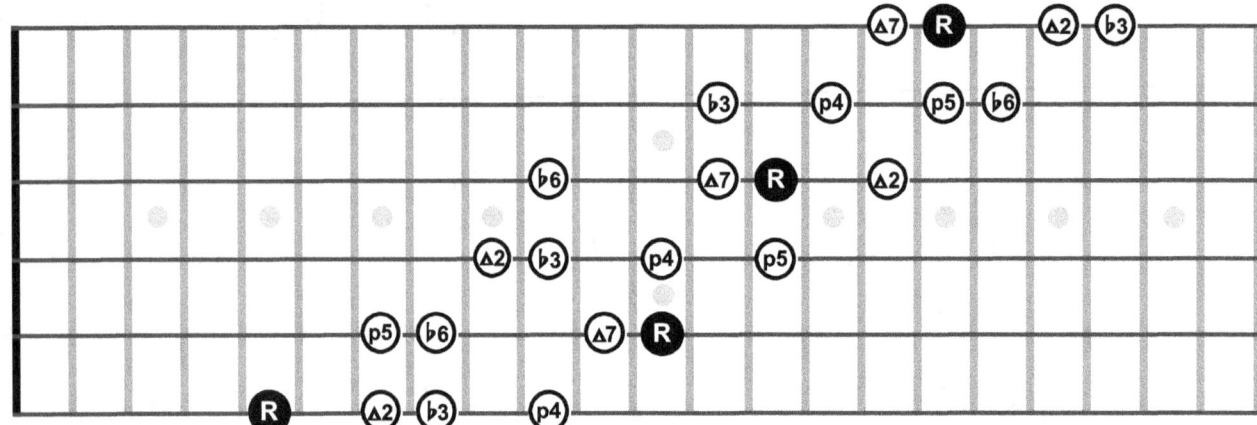

A Locrian #6 Scale

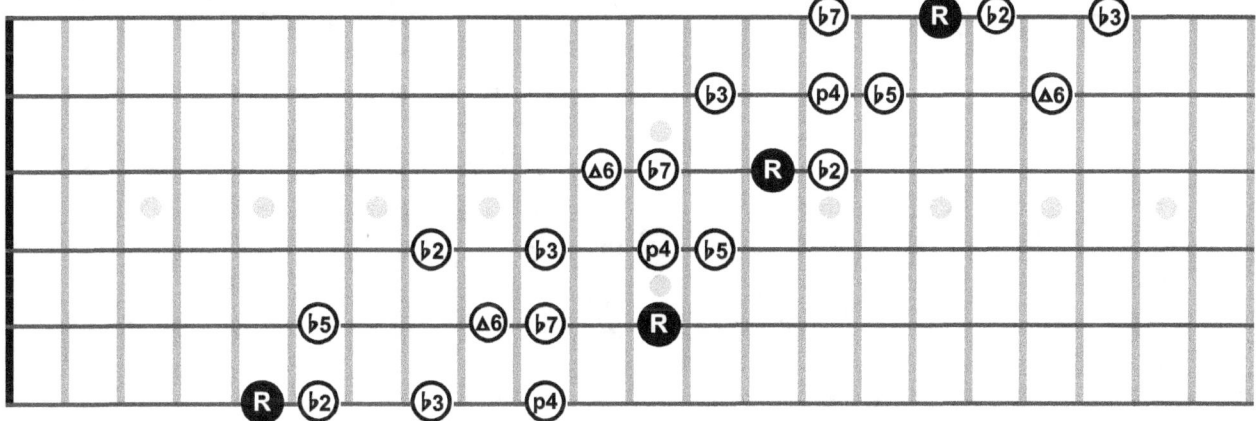

A Ionian Augmented Scale

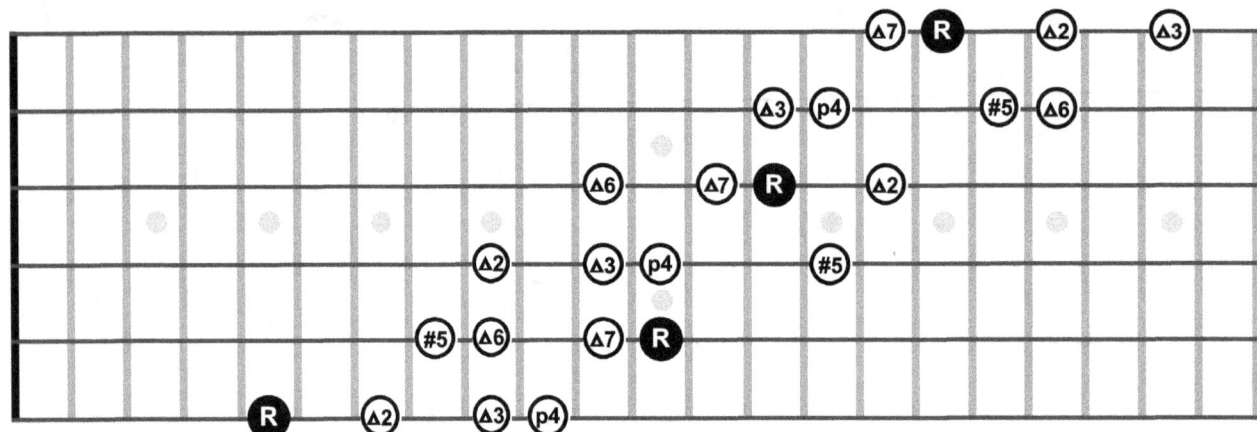

A Dorian #4 Scale

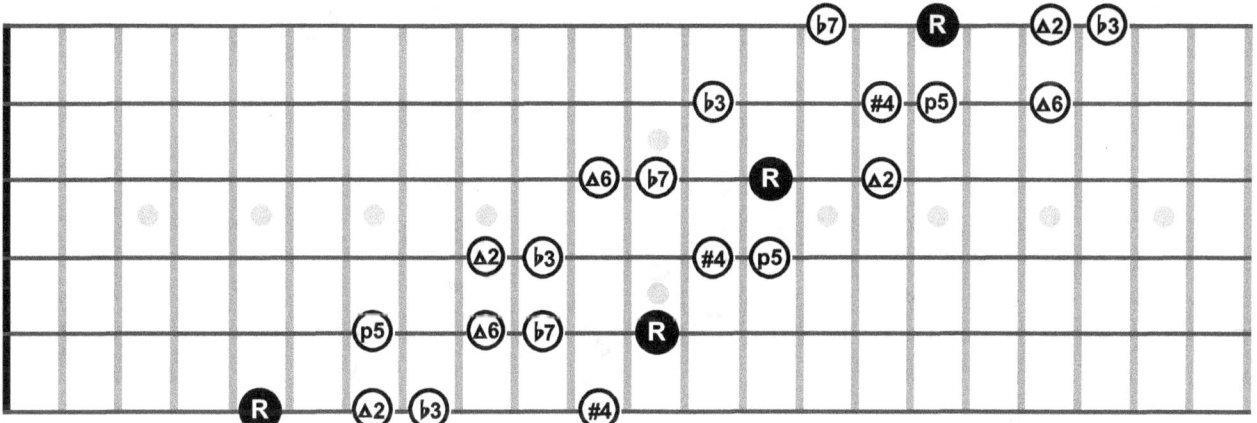

A Phrygian Dominant Scale

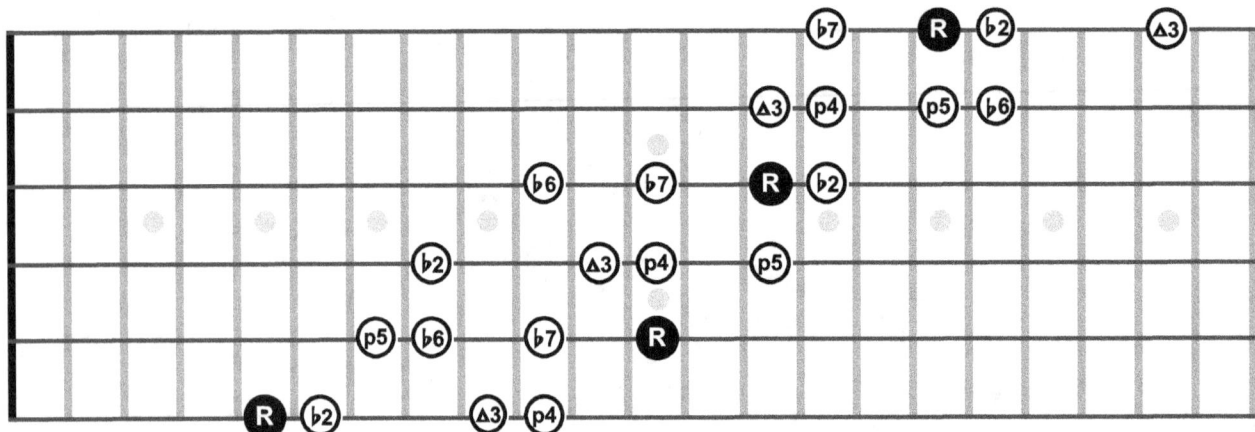

A Lydian #2 Scale

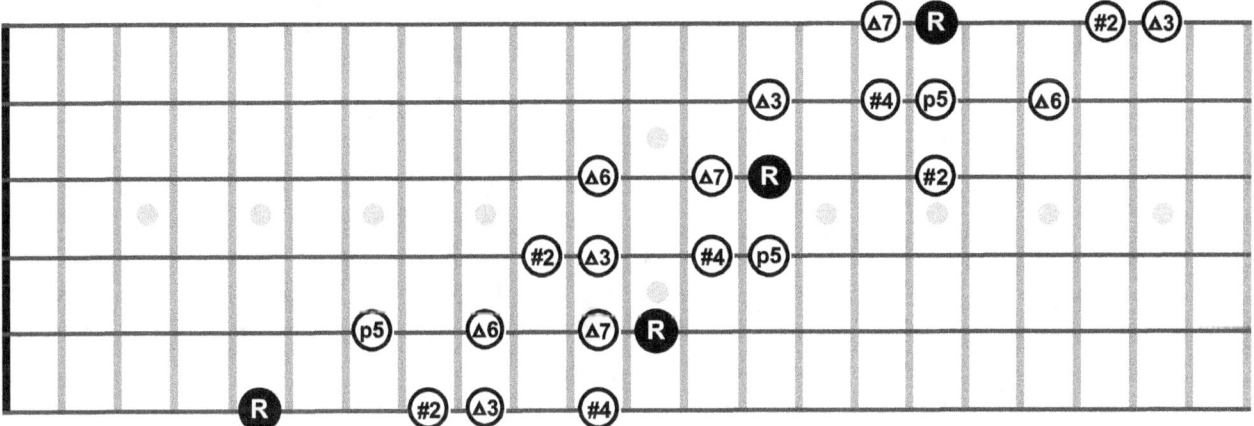

A Ultralocrian Scale

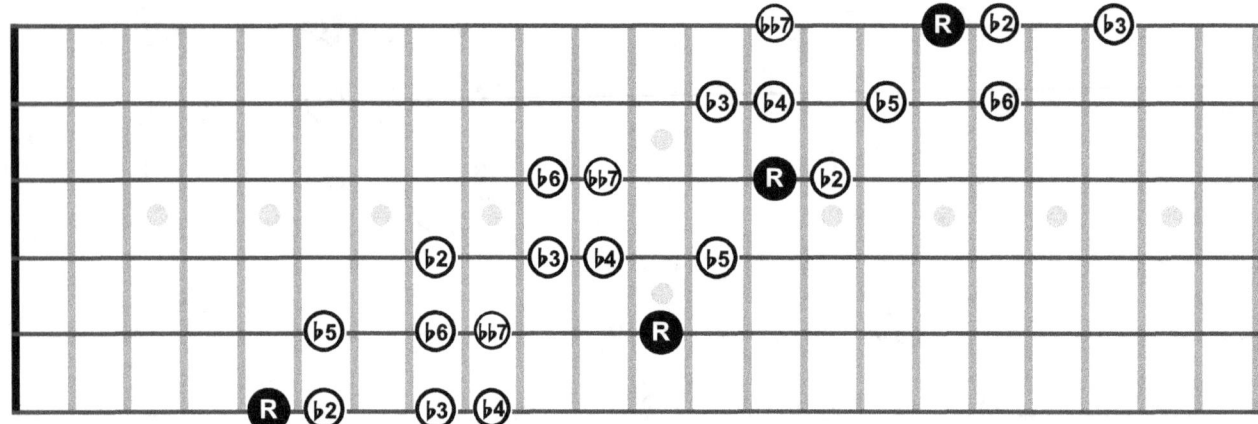

A Melodic Minor Scale

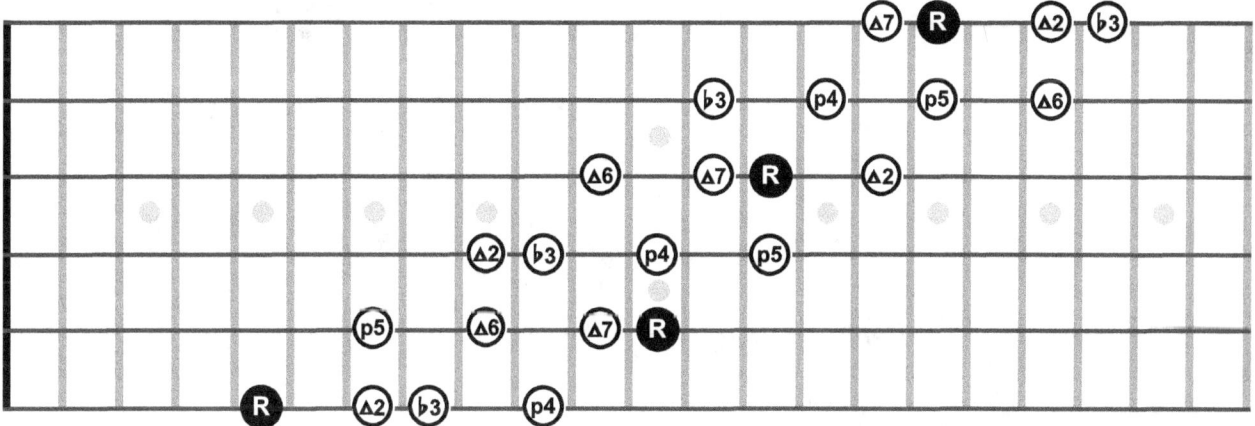

A Dorian b2 Scale

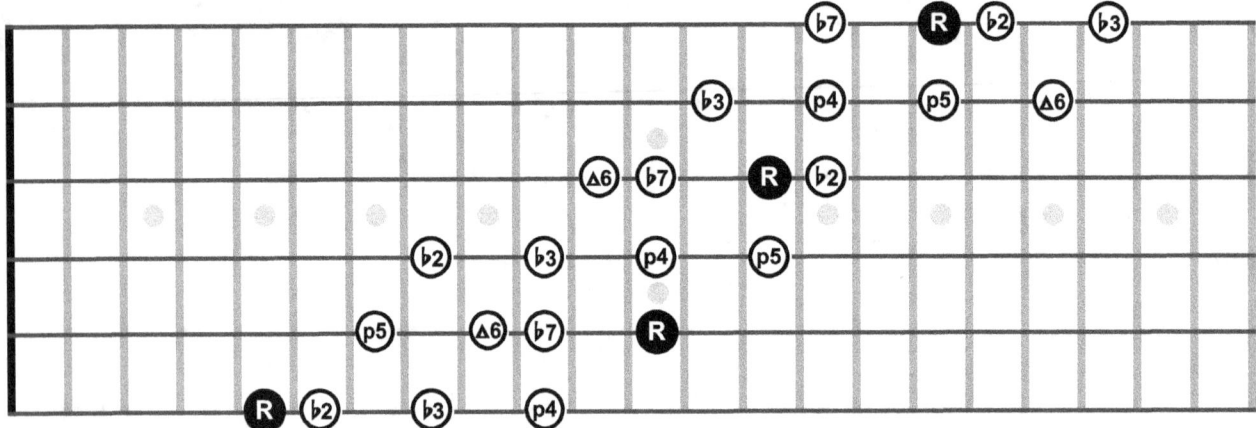

A Lydian Augmented Scale

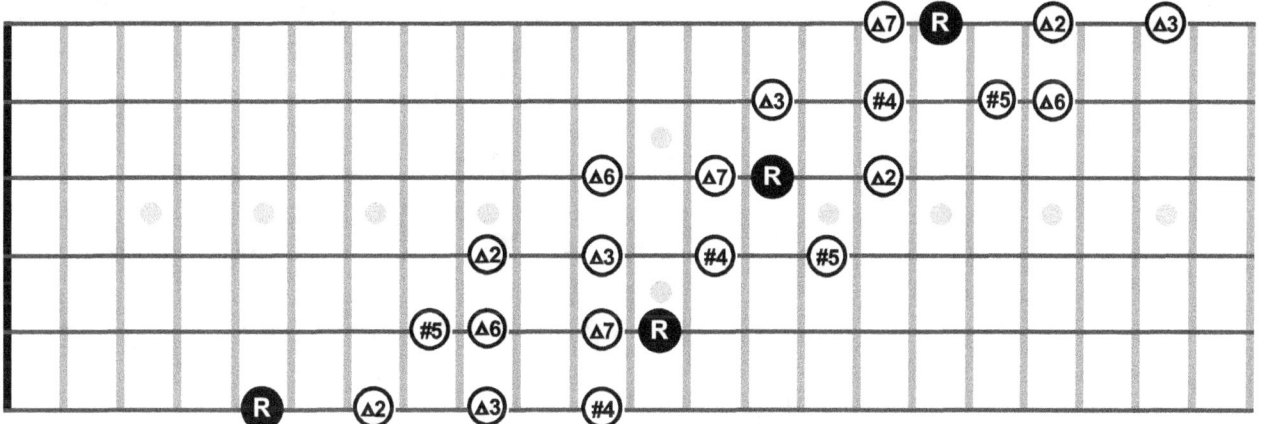

A Lydian Dominant Scale

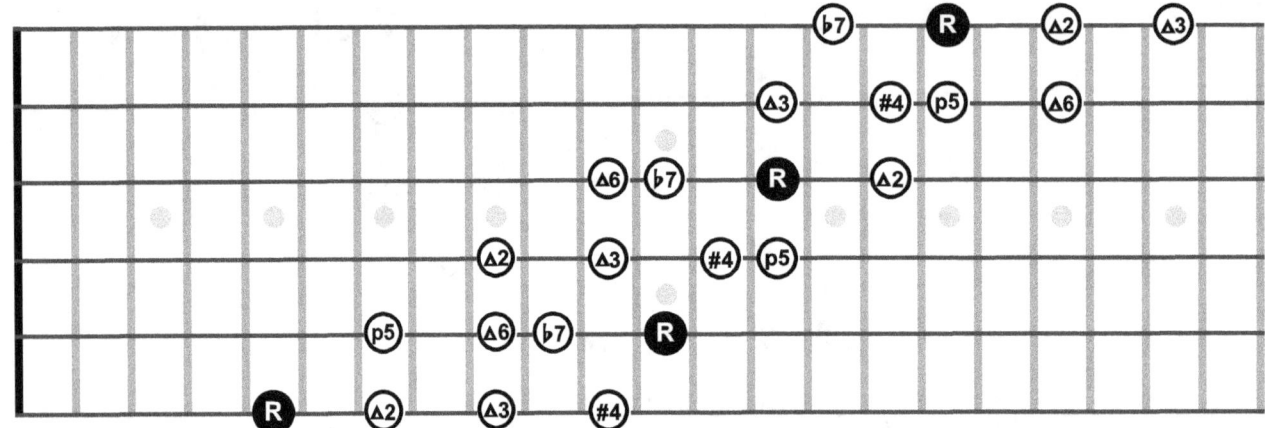

A Mixolydian b6 Scale

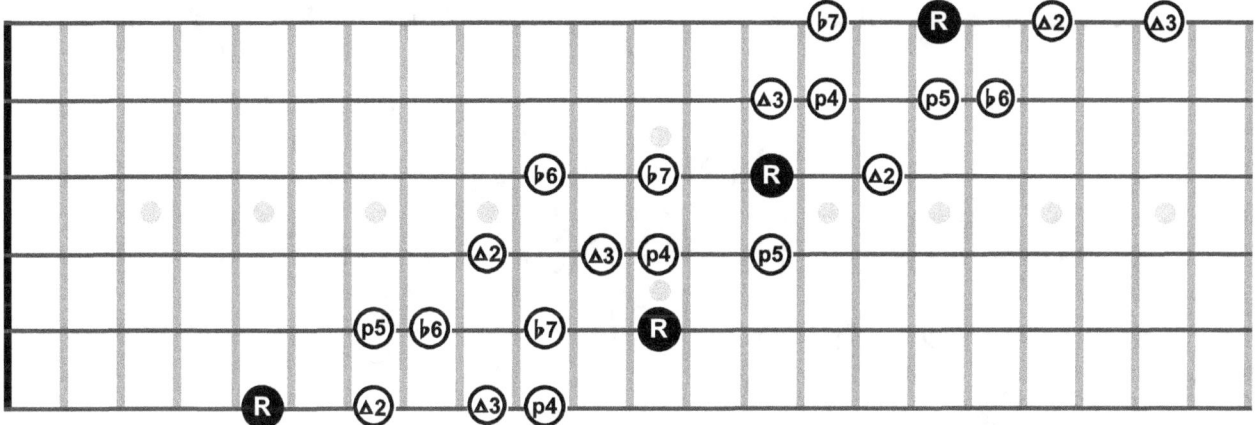

A Locrian #2 Scale

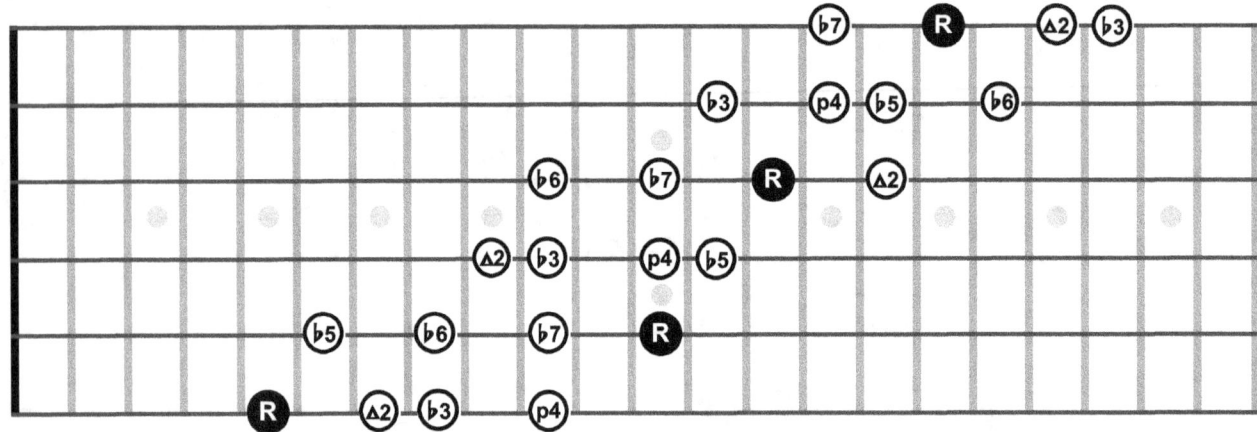

A Altered Scale

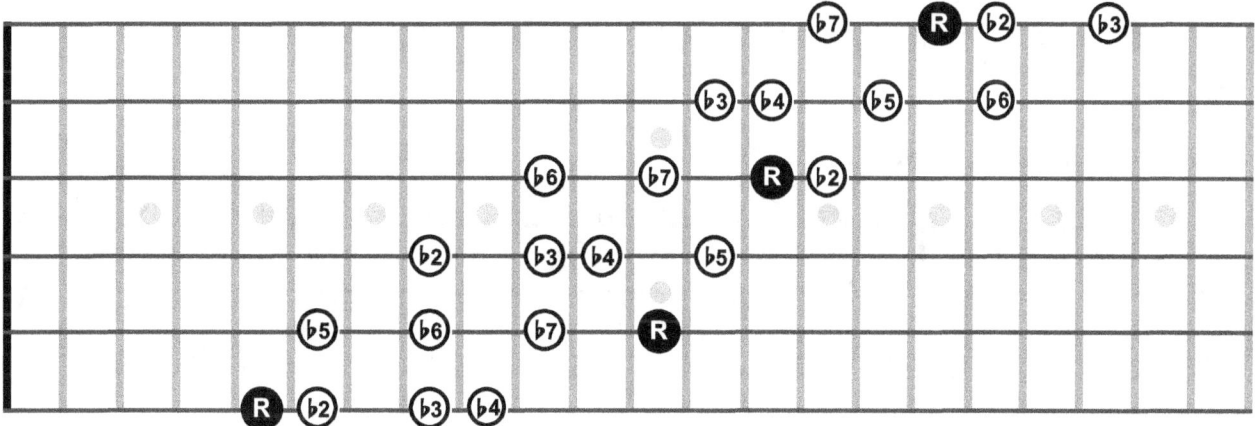

A Major Arpeggio

Shape 1

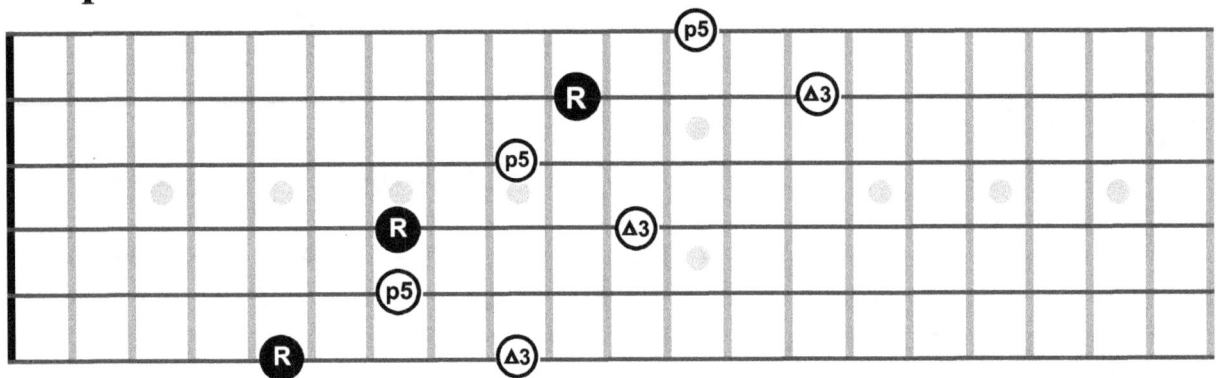

Shape 2

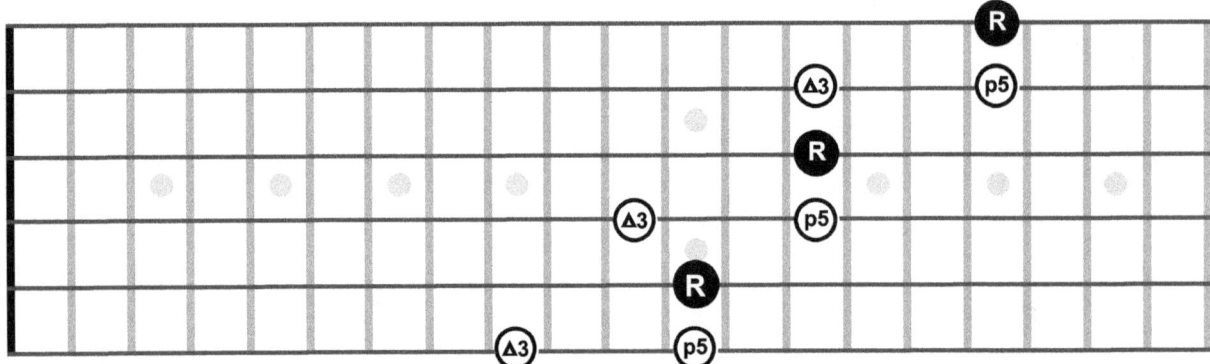

Shape 3

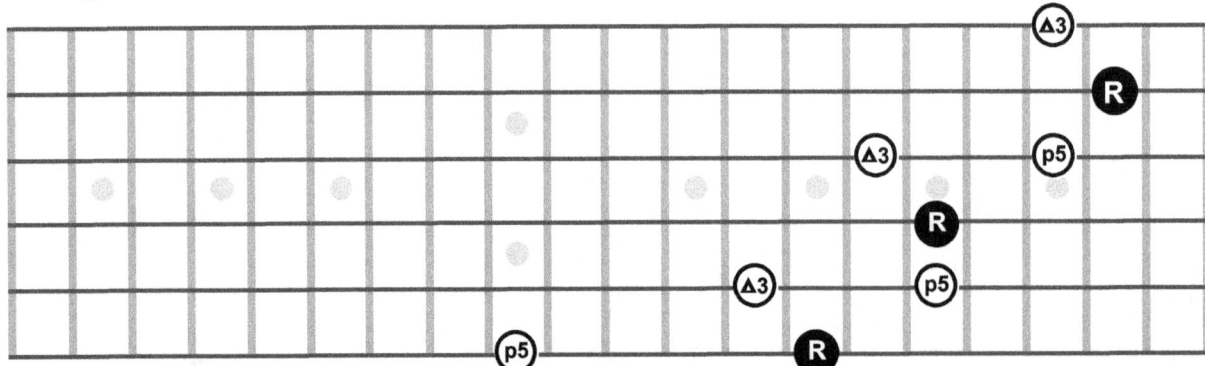

A Minor Arpeggio

Shape 1

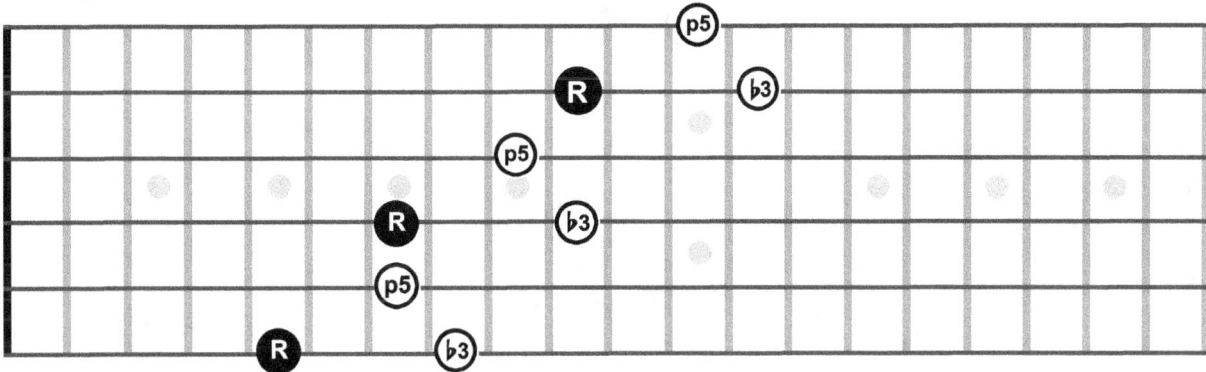

Shape 2

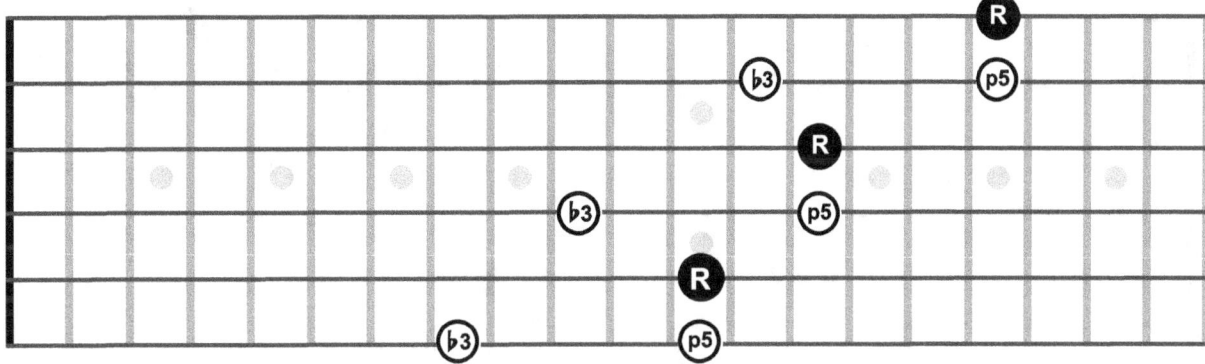

Shape 3

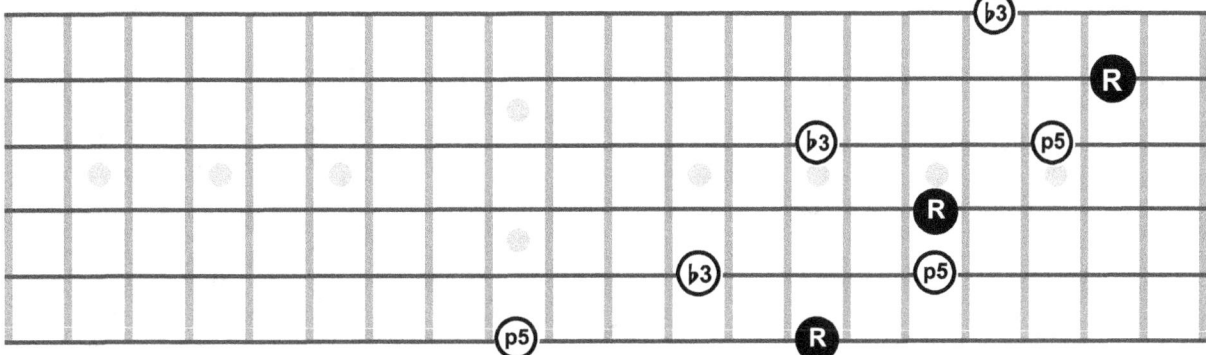

A Augmented Arpeggio

Shape 1

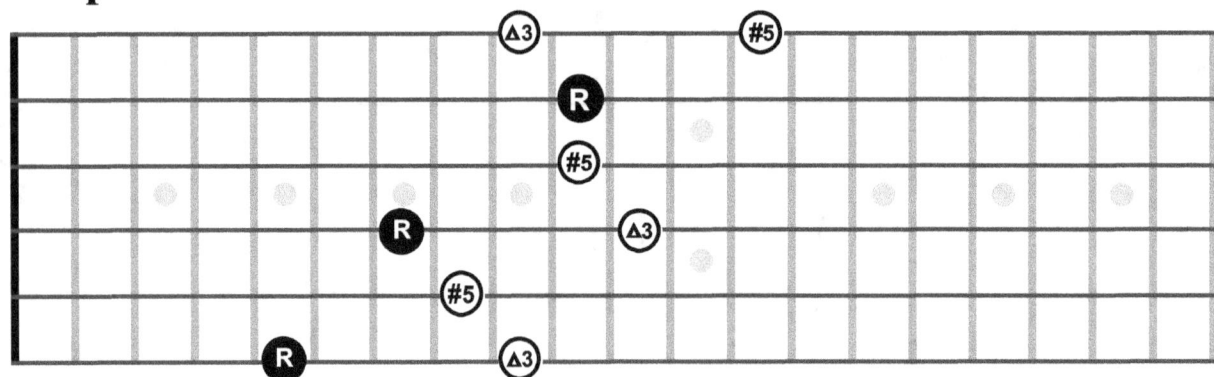

Shape 2

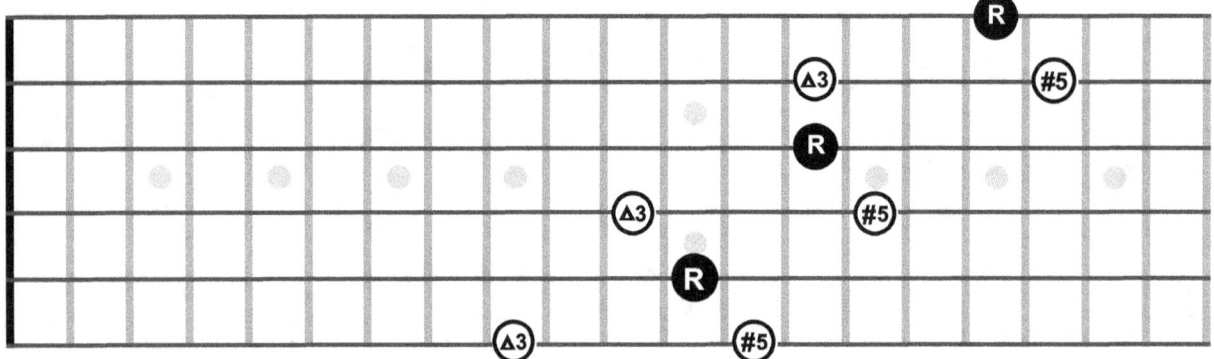

Shape 3

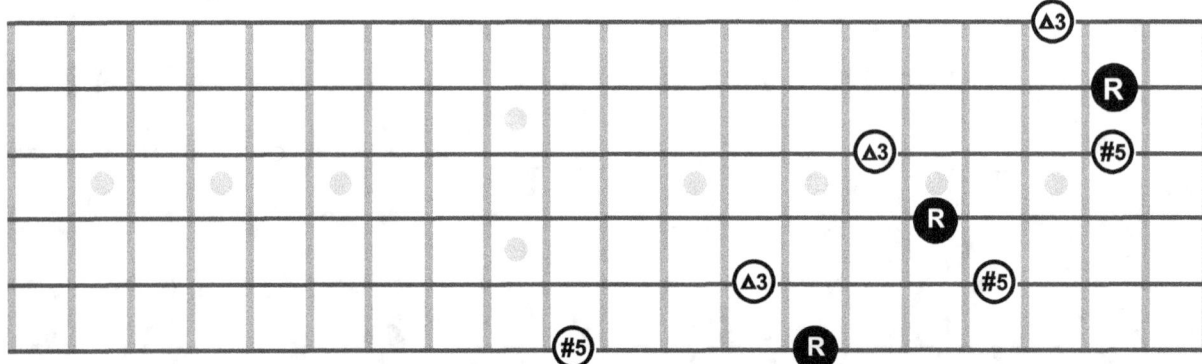

A Diminished Arpeggio

Shape 1

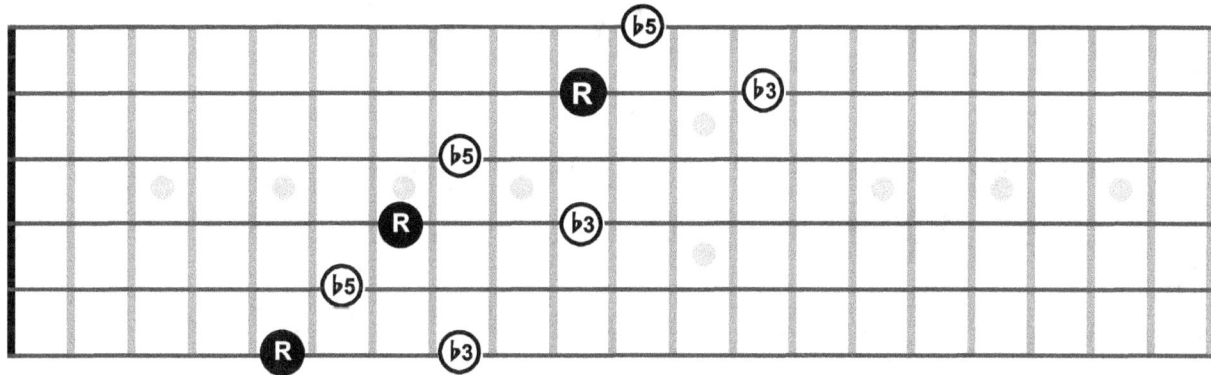

Shape 2

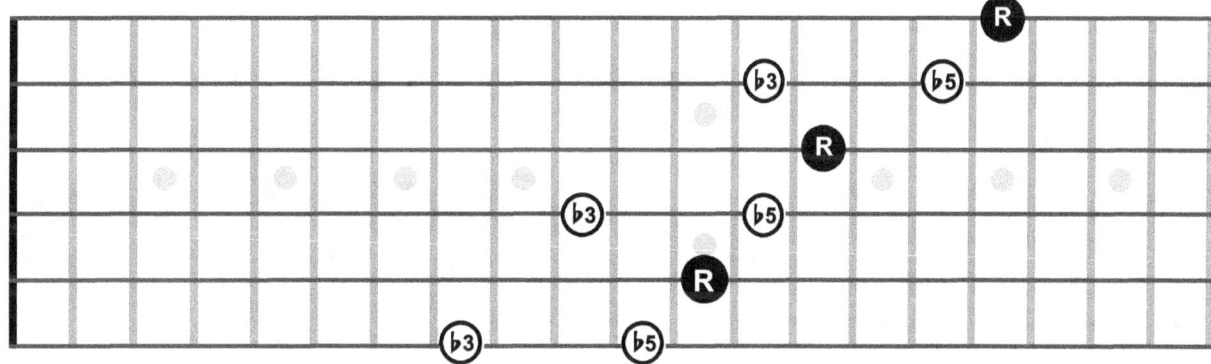

Shape 3

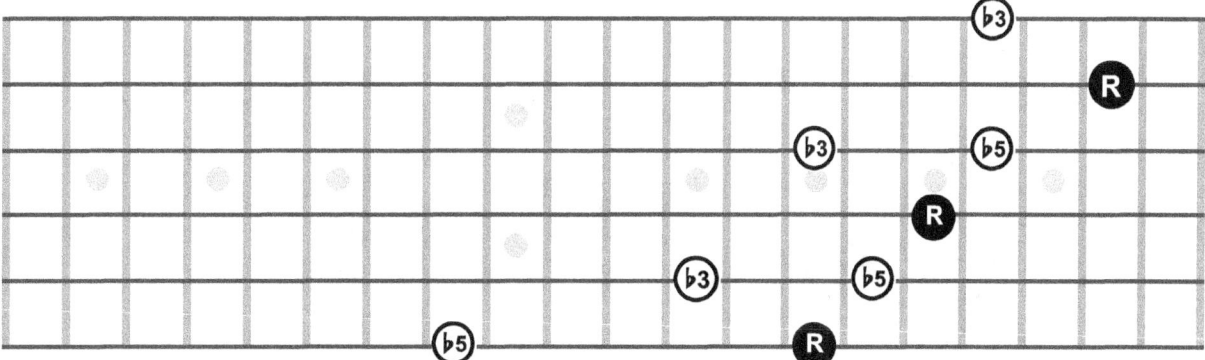

A Major 7 Arpeggio

Shape 1

Shape 2

Shape 3

Shape 4

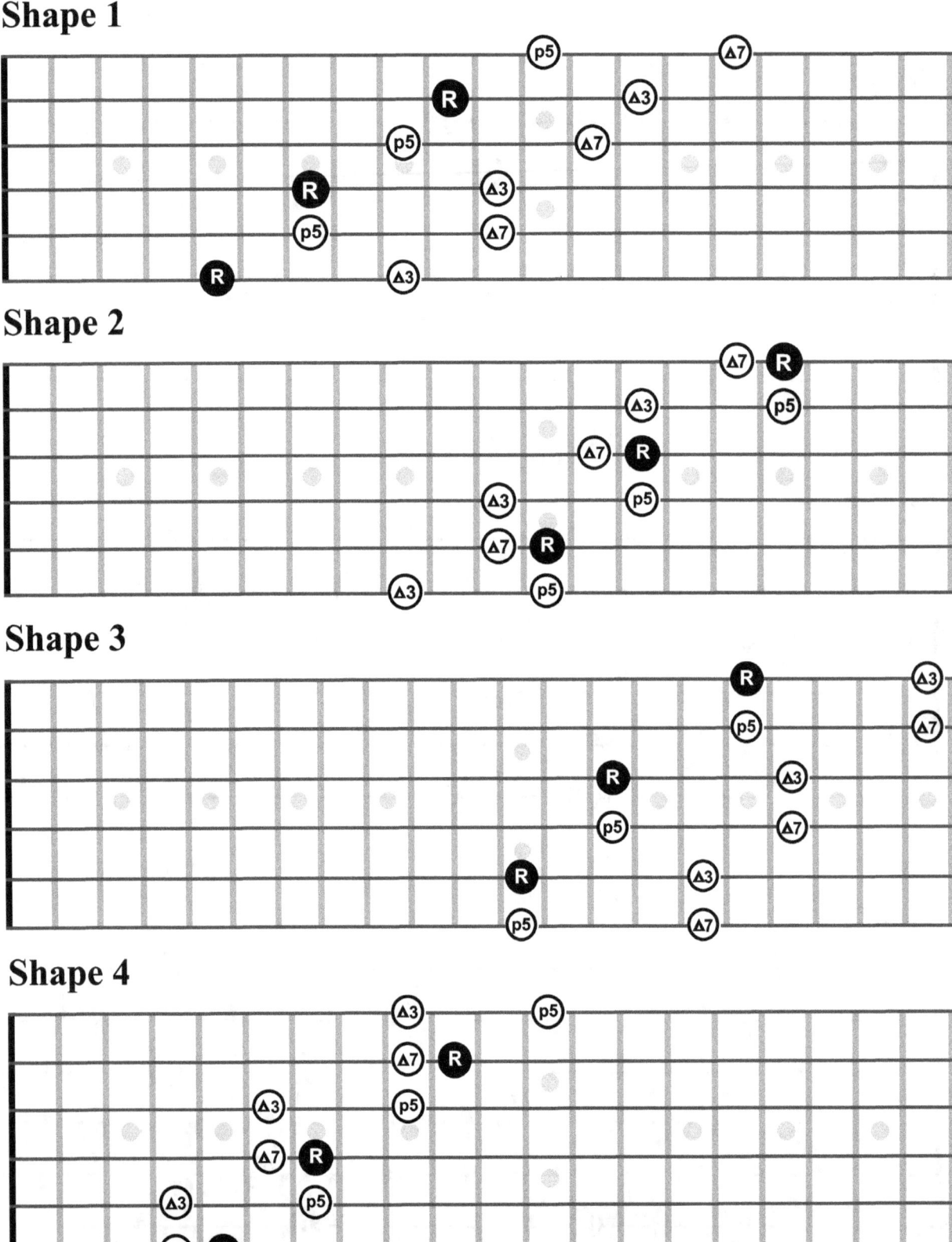

A Minor 7 Arpeggio

Shape 1

Shape 2

Shape 3

Shape 4

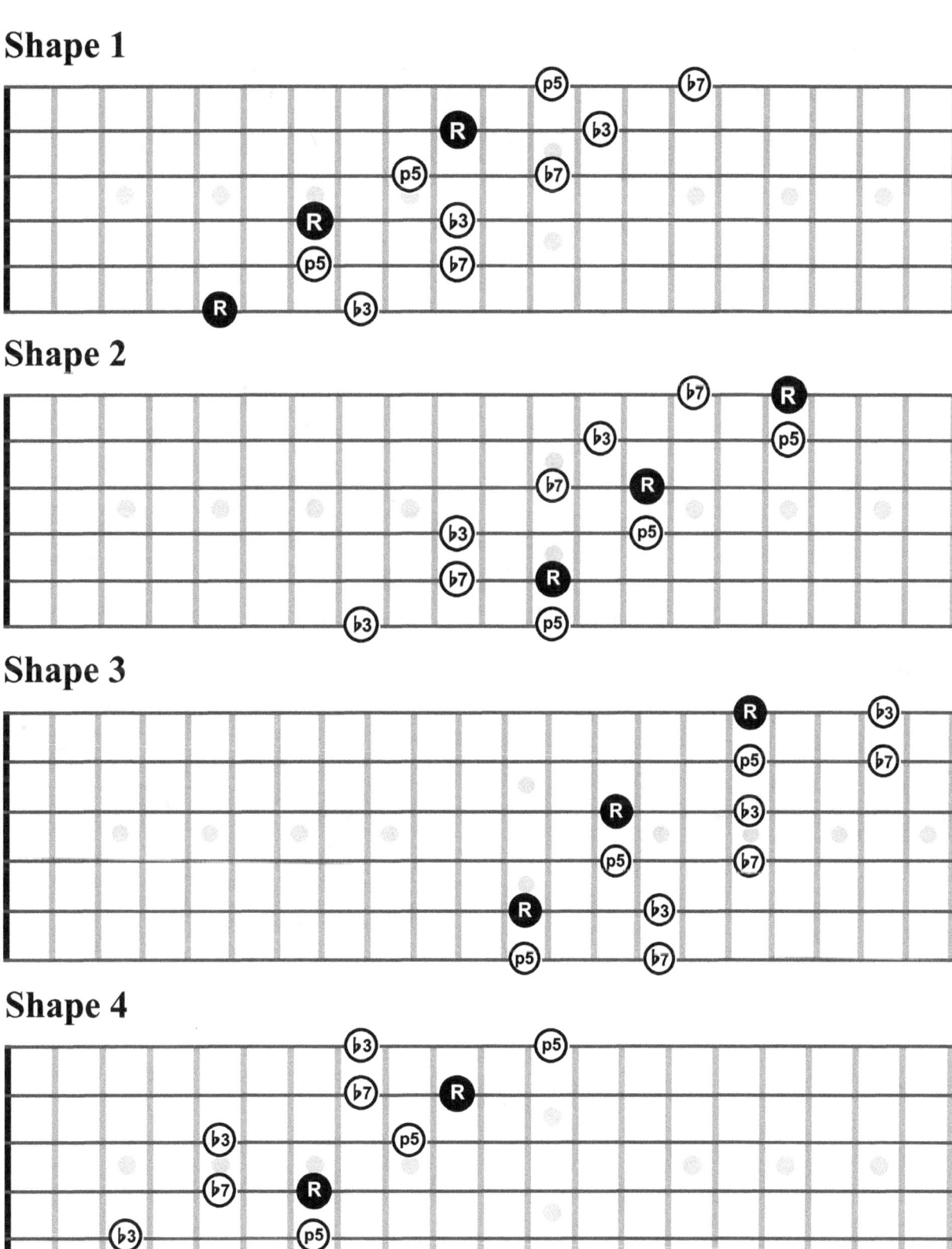

A Dominant 7 Arpeggio

Shape 1

Shape 2

Shape 3

Shape 4

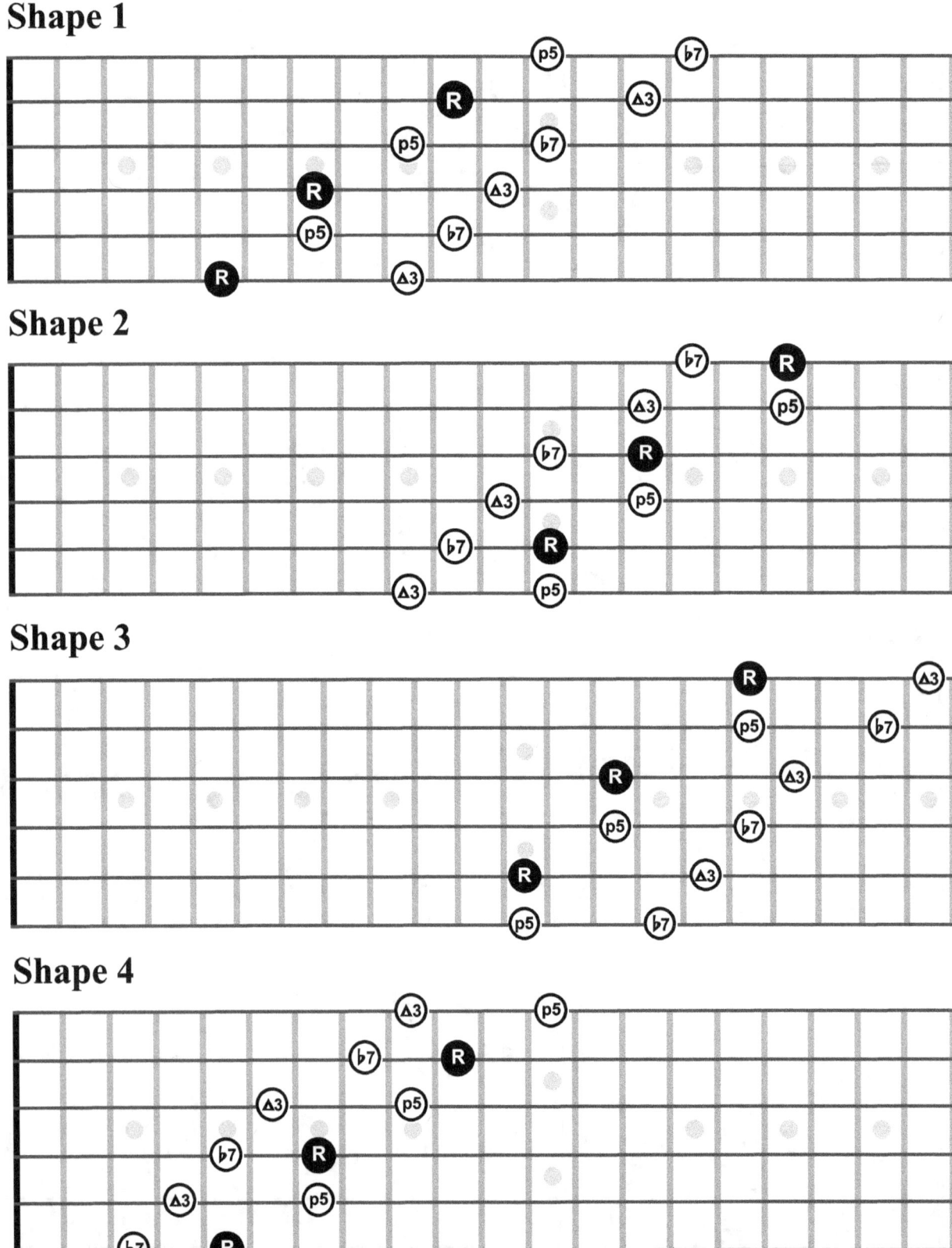

A Minor/Major 7 Arpeggio

Shape 1

Shape 2

Shape 3

Shape 4

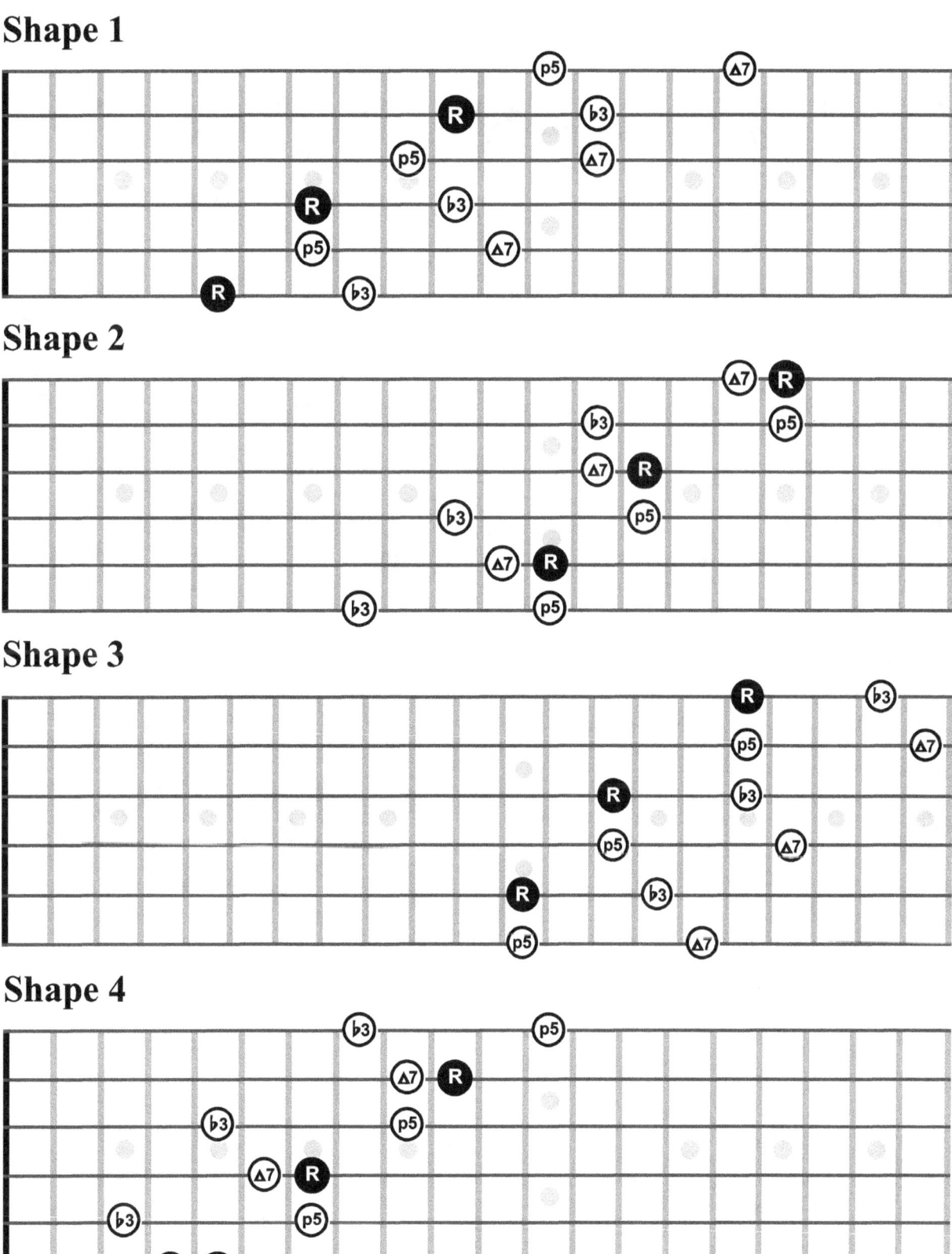

A Major 7#5 Arpeggio

Shape 1

Shape 2

Shape 3

Shape 4

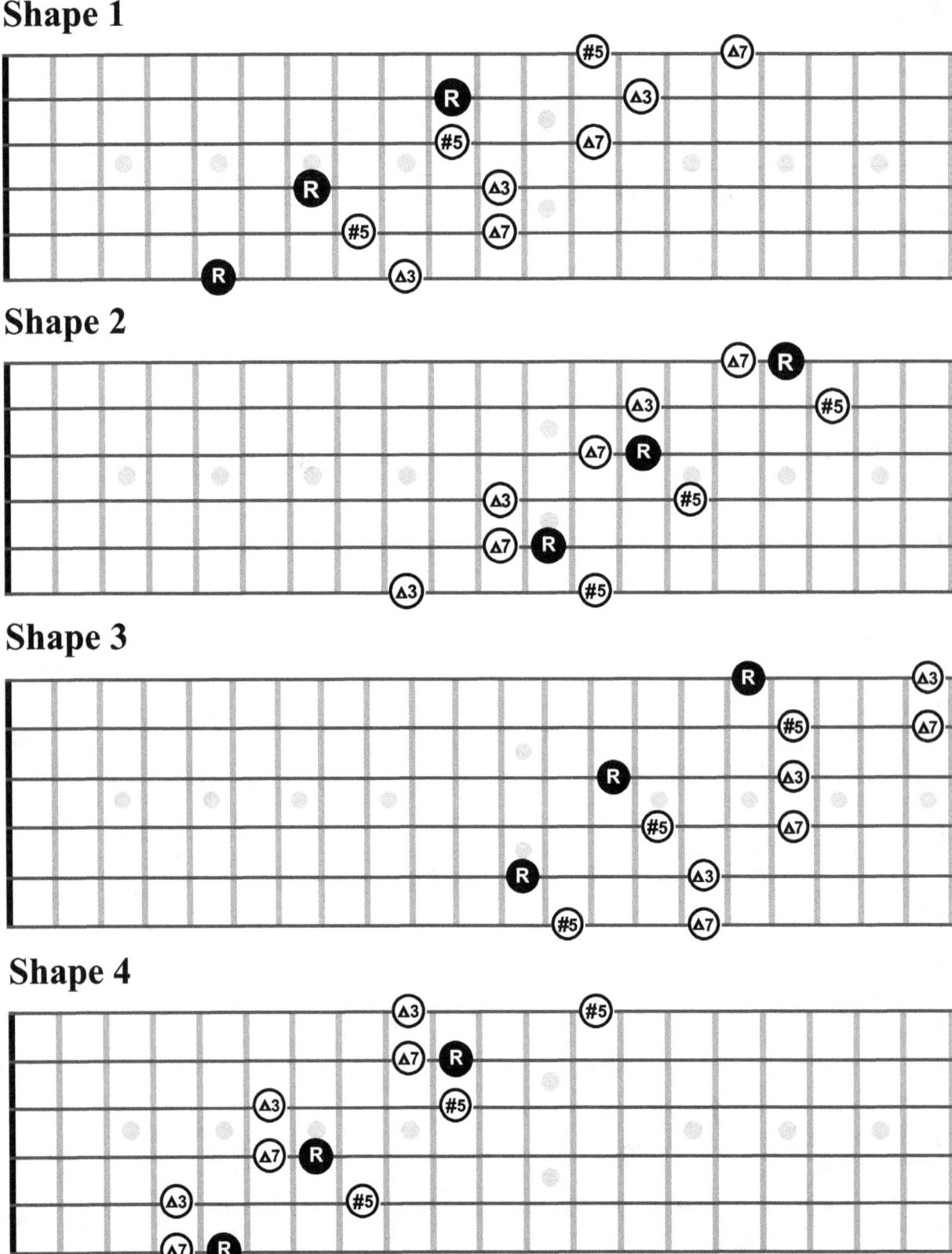

A Minor 7b5 Arpeggio

Shape 1

Shape 2

Shape 3

Shape 4

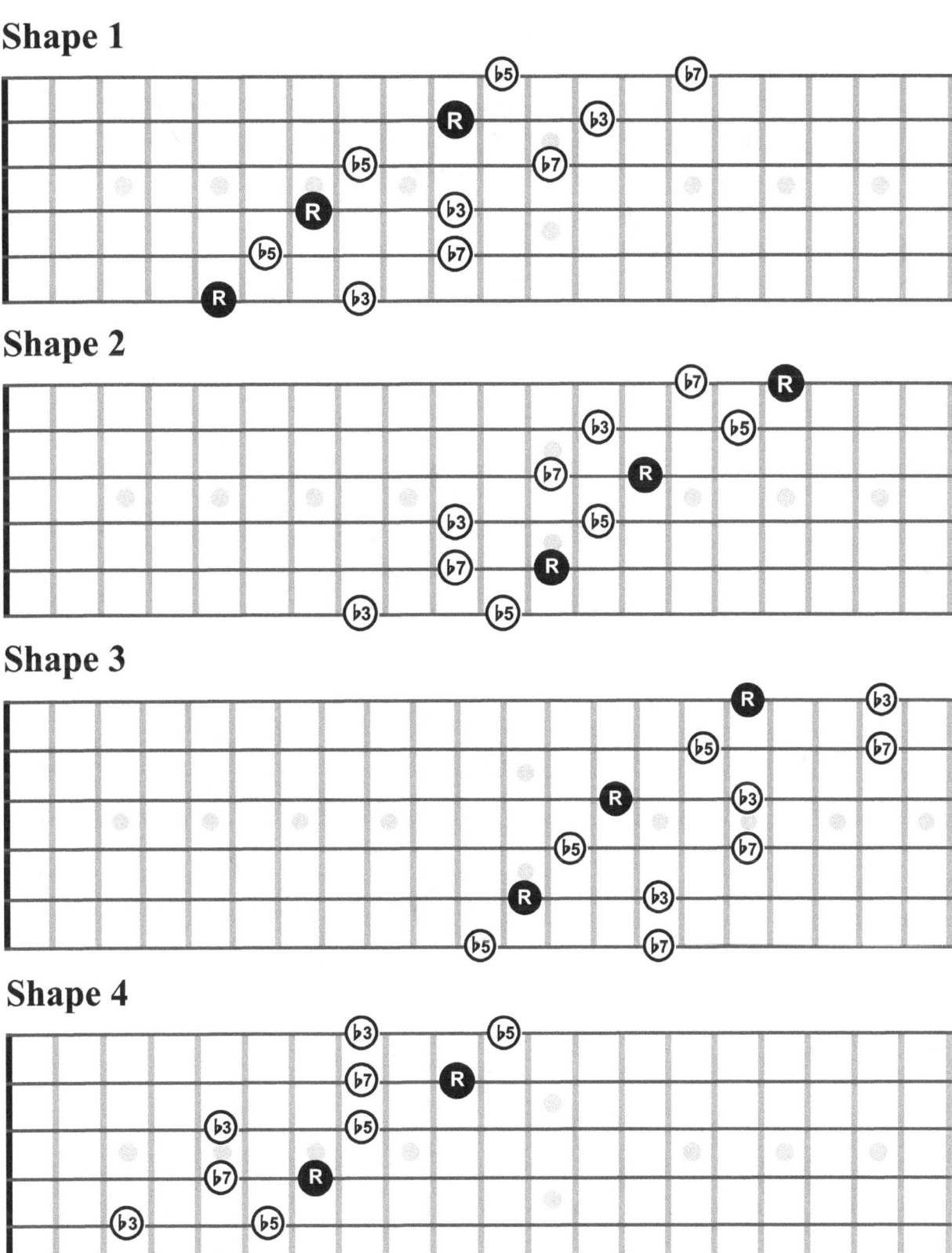

A Diminished 7 Arpeggio

Shape 1

Shape 2

Shape 3

Shape 4

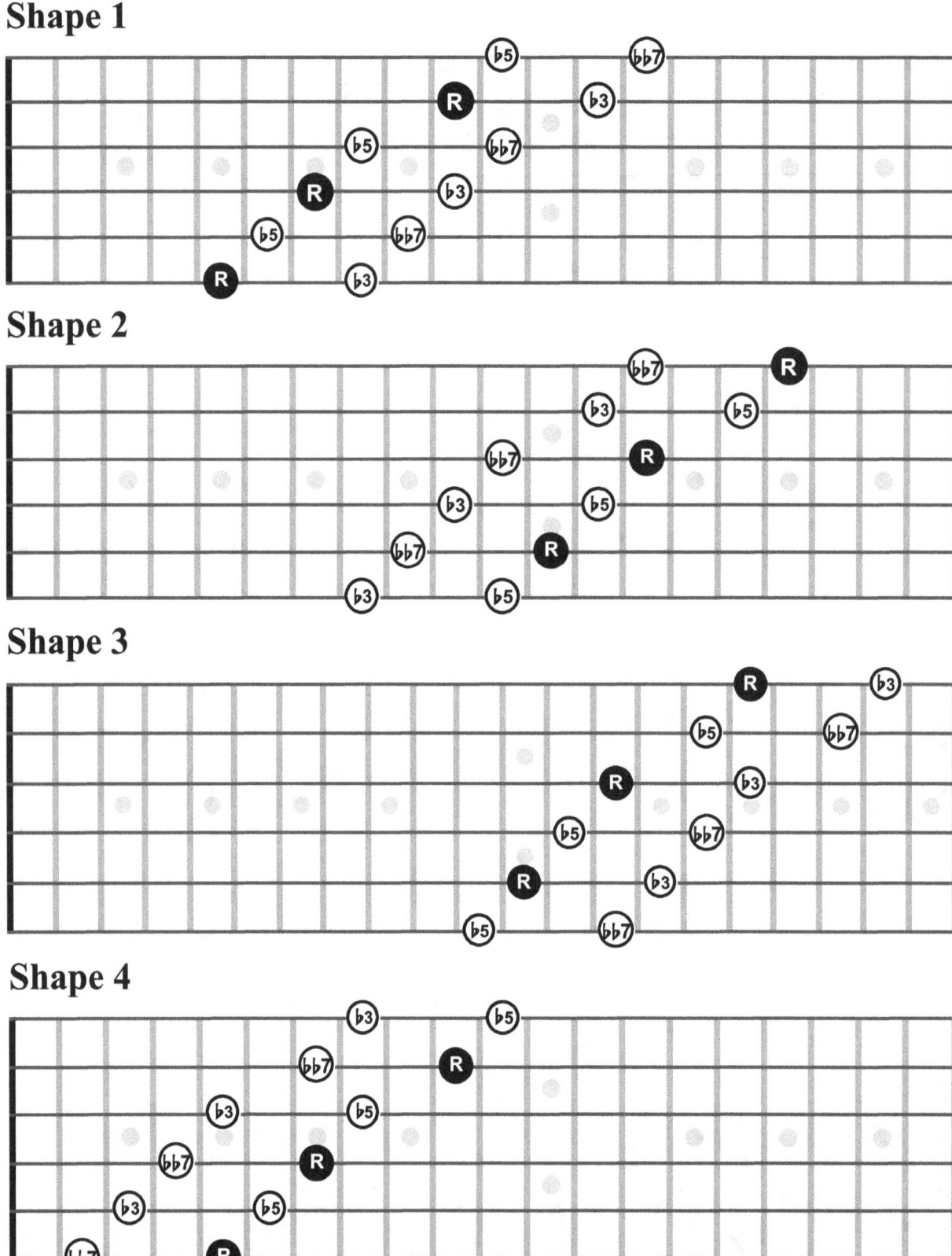

www.ingramcontent.com/pod-product-compliance
Lightning Source LLC
Chambersburg PA
CBHW081202280526
45791CB00006B/2160